Knowing Jesus in the Power of His Resurrection

by

Sara Gibson

Fairmont Books is a ministry of The McDougal Foundation, Inc., a Maryland nonprofit corporation dedicated to spreading the Gospel of the Lord Jesus Christ to as many people as possible in the shortest time possible.

Published by:

𝒥airmont Books

P.O. Box 3595
Hagerstown, MD   21742-3595
www.mcdougalpublishing.com

ISBN 1-58158-034-7

Printed in the United States of America
For Worldwide Distribution

Dedication

I dedicate this book to my husband Buddy. I want to honor him because he is such a great man. After all, he "gave" me to the ministry.

Acknowledgments

I give much praise and thanksgiving to God for McDougal Publishing and for Harold McDougal, who worked with me to make this book possible.

Contents

Foreword

Far too much attention is being paid these days in many Christian circles to Satan, as if he were someone extremely important. He's not. Precisely because the enemy is determined to be the center of our attention, we must see to it that he is not – ever. He is not worthy of the time and effort many are giving him.

Our Lord Jesus, who is sending great revival into our midst, is, and must be, our focus. When we give Him the attention He deserves, all evil influences take flight. They cannot stand in His presence. He is Lord of all lords and God over all gods, and there is none beside Him.

This is the refreshing emphasis of Sara Gibson's *After the Cross.* She shows us that the price has been paid and the sacrifice has been given for our complete deliverance. To ignore the benefits of the cross is to "crucify [our Lord] afresh and put Him to an open shame." It is with pride that we bring this timely book to print.

Harold McDougal
Hagerstown, Maryland

Introduction

Every teacher and preacher seems to be given a special theme by God. Lately, my assignment has been preaching Jesus and the power of His resurrection. I find it amazing to contemplate all that Christ has already accomplished on the cross for me and how I can appropriate it in my daily life. Not only has He provided much that we have not yet moved into, but He is also living to minister to us NOW. Many Christians have not yet realized this fact or taken advantage of it.

I have been preaching the Word of God now for many years, but some very new and special things have been happening recently on the inside of me. God is showing me truths in His Word that are transforming my own spiritual life and enabling me to reach out and bless many others as well.

There has never been a time like this one, and I am excited, not only to be alive today, but also to have a part in what God is doing in His Kingdom in the hearts of men and women all around the world. As we are hungering for Him, He is filling us – as He promised. Still, many hang back, not realizing all that is theirs as believers. This book is an effort to address that lack.

Because I have a teaching anointing, I am often compelled to begin at the beginning, and I ask those whom I am teaching to be patient with me and to allow me to lay a proper foundation for what is to come.

I can only share what the Lord has done in my own life, the way He has led me. His truths have changed my own life, and I believe that they will change yours too. His Word has prepared me for life in the heavenlies, and it will do the same for others.

I trust that you will be blessed and lifted into a new spiritual level by the pages of *After the Cross*.

Sara Gibson
Meridian, Mississippi

Yea doubtless, and I count all things but loss for the excellency of the knowledge of Christ Jesus my Lord: for whom I have suffered the loss of all things, and do count them but dung, that I may win Christ, and be found in him, not having mine own righteousness, which is of the law, but that which is through the faith of Christ, the righteousness which is of God by faith: THAT I MAY KNOW HIM, AND THE POWER OF HIS RESURRECTION, and the fellowship of his sufferings, being made conformable unto his death.

Philippians 3:8-10

Part I:

What It Means to Know Jesus in the Power of His Resurrection

Chapter One

Paul's Desire

Yea doubtless, and I count all things but loss for the excellency of the knowledge of Christ Jesus my Lord: for whom I have suffered the loss of all things, and DO COUNT THEM BUT DUNG, that I may win Christ, and be found in him, not having mine own righteousness, which is of the law, but that which is through the faith of Christ, the righteousness which is of God by faith: That I may know him, and the power of his resurrection, and the fellowship of his sufferings, being made conformable unto his death.

Philippians 3:8-10

The apostle Paul was probably the best educated man of his day, at least in religious circles. After all, he went to the best Bible school around.

Paul, however, had a lot more than that going for him. He came from one of the best families and, therefore; he had the best pedigree. He spoke many languages, he held the coveted Roman citizenship by birth, he was part of an elite group within Judaism, and he was more zealous than all of his companions. But what did Paul say about his advantaged life, his vast natural knowledge and his high social and religious standing? Shockingly, he said, *"I count them but dung."*

Most of us know what dung is. It is waste, feces, manure. The New Living Bible calls it *"garbage,"* but this was the worst kind of garbage. How shocking! Paul compared the advantages of his life to *"dung."* Why would he do that?

We can understand this utterly shocking statement better if we look at exactly what Paul was speaking about, what he was comparing his standing in life with. What was it that Paul would much rather have than everything his privileged position in life afforded? The cry of his heart was: *"that I might know Him and the power of His resurrection."* To the apostle Paul, who was, in my estimation, one of the greatest men who ever lived, nothing was more important than knowing Christ in a fuller and richer way and understanding all the benefits of His sacrifice on Calvary.

Paul wrote more than half of the New Testament, just as Moses wrote much of the Old Testament. God used these two men more than most others in history. What Paul considered to be important, therefore, is very important to me, and I pay attention to it. If it was important to Paul, then it is also important to me.

I am sad to say, however, in the early years of the twenty-first century, that a great many Christians still do not know Christ in the power of His resurrection. Far too many Christians alive today, even Spirit-filled believers, are not living any higher than the saints of the Old Testament lived in their day.

The children of Israel had many good things going for them in Old Testament times. They already had forgiveness of sins through the shedding of the blood of animals. They were God's people, too. They were already experiencing miracles. They were already receiving healings. They already had a promise of provision, and God often did very unusual miracles to provide their physical needs. There were even cases of the dead being raised to life again in those days.

Those were great days, but what we are promised through Christ is so much better that there is no comparison. It is true that many Christians have risen to the same levels as the saints of old, but not many have gone higher. The Old Testament, however, only held types and shadows of that which was to come, and now we are living in the time of the real thing:

> *But now hath he obtained a more excellent ministry, by how much also he is the mediator of a better covenant, which was established upon better promises.* Hebrews 8:6

If Paul could take all the privilege of his birth, his education and his experience and *"count it but dung,"* that must mean there was something awfully important to be known, and He wanted to know it. The benefits of Calvary are so vast and deep that we have only begun to plumb them. Each of us should have this desire to discover the benefits that the death and resurrection of the Lord Jesus Christ have provided for us and to have them realized in our own lives.

I am personally convinced that this is where the Church, as a whole, needs to go today. If knowing Jesus in the power of His resurrection is this beneficial, then we need to go after it. We need to experience it. We need to press in to it until we receive its benefit.

On Calvary, Christ suffered for us, and now we don't have to suffer. He paid the price, and now we don't have to pay. He did the work, and now we can enjoy all the benefits of it — if we know what those benefits are.

So many of us are trying to fight battles that have already been won. We are trying to do what has already been done. We are asking God to repeat what does not need repeating. The work is done. It is time that we rejoice in it and that we take advantage of it.

A battle cannot be more finished than finished. A provision cannot be more made than made. An enemy cannot be more defeated than defeated. Satan is defeated. He is dethroned. He is spoiled. He is disarmed. All of his authority has been taken away from him. That's the Gospel, the Good News from God, that Jesus has totally defeated the enemy.

Jesus has died to the world for me. Jesus has died to the flesh for me. I'm risen with Jesus, and I am made to reign with Him.

I personally want to enjoy all the benefits the Lord purchased for me on Calvary. I want to have all that His death and resurrection afford. When we have sufficient understanding of what Jesus has already accomplished for us in His death and resurrection, we will have a more complete victory.

Why is it that many Christians are satisfied just to have fire insurance? If they can stay out of Hell, they're happy. That's as far as they care to go. But there is so much more. God's will for us is that we walk in daily victory and blessing, and we can – because, in the resurrection, Jesus defeated Satan forever.

Satan is totally defeated. Jesus paralyzed him, demoted him, defanged him, disarmed him and made him of no effect. This is the message of the glorious Gospel of the Lord Jesus Christ, and more people need to hear it, believe it and act on it.

Chapter Two

Moses' Sin

Wherefore the people did chide with Moses, and said, Give us water that we may drink. And Moses said unto them, Why chide ye with me? wherefore do ye tempt the LORD? And the people thirsted there for water; and the people murmured against Moses, and said, Wherefore is this that thou hast brought us up out of Egypt, to kill us and our children and our cattle with thirst?

Exodus 17:2-3

After the children of Israel came out of Egypt and crossed the Red Sea, they came to a place in the wilderness where there was no water for them to drink. This was serious, because water was their life, and without it, they would all quickly die.

Rather than turn to God and seek Him, however, the people turned on Moses. This word *chide* means "to murmur and find fault." The Israelites were lifting themselves up in pride against God and His appointed leader, and this led them to murmur and find fault.

Moses cried out to the Lord for help, and the Lord answered him:

> *And the LORD said unto Moses, Go on before the people, and take with thee of the elders of Israel; and thy rod, wherewith thou smotest the river, take in thine hand, and go. Behold, I will stand before thee there upon the rock in Horeb; and thou shalt smite the rock, and there shall come water out of it, that the people may drink. And Moses did so in the sight of the elders of Israel.*
> Exodus 17:5-6

When Moses struck the rock, water came out of it, and the thirst of the people was quenched. God had allowed this situation to come into their lives to prove His power and His ability to supply for them – even in a barren place.

The children of Israel had no reason to doubt God or to murmur and complain about His designated leadership, but they apparently did not learn that lesson well enough. A similar situation arose later in another place. Again the people found themselves in a barren area of the desert of Zin, and again they began to murmur against Moses and Aaron. God told Moses to do almost exactly the same thing again, to stand before the rock, but this time, to speak to it. If he would do this, the Lord showed him, water would come forth from the rock to quench the thirst of the people.

Moses was very discouraged by the reaction of the people. He couldn't understand why they hadn't learned their lesson. He was so angry that, although he seemingly obeyed the Lord as before, we see that he did not do it wholeheartedly or exactly as God had directed:

> *And Moses took the rod from before the LORD, as he commanded him. And Moses and Aaron gathered the congregation together before the rock, and he said unto them, Hear now, ye rebels; must we fetch you water out of this rock? And Moses lifted up his hand, and with his rod he smote the rock twice: and the water came out abundantly, and the congregation drank, and their beasts also.*
>
> Numbers 20:9-11

The result of Moses' action was good, as before, but something was very different this time. This time the Lord was angry with His two servants, Moses and Aaron, and spoke very harshly with them:

> *And the LORD spake unto Moses and Aaron, Because ye believed me not, to sanctify me in the eyes of the children of Israel, therefore ye shall not bring*

Moses' Sin

*this congregation into the land which I have given
them.*   Numbers 20:12

For the longest time, I had a problem understanding this passage. The Scriptures show us that Moses was the meekest man on the face of the earth, that he was God's chosen deliverer, that God used him to give us a great portion of the Holy Scriptures, that signs and wonders and miracles were manifested through him on a very regular basis, that he saw into the heavenlies and supernaturally received the pattern for the wilderness Tabernacle, and that he even talked with God *"face to face"* (Exodus 33:11). Why on earth would Moses receive such a harsh judgment and be prevented from even entering the Promised Land? And for something as simple as this?

Moses had faced down Pharaoh and won freedom for all his people, and when most of the children of Israel had begun to murmur at the Red Sea, he had remained strong in his faith. But now, because he struck the rock twice rather than speaking to it, he would miss the Promised Land. That seemed very harsh to me.

And what about Aaron? While Moses was up on the mountain in the glory cloud of God's presence receiving the Ten Commandments for the people, Aaron had been building a golden calf for them to worship. It is a good thing that I wasn't God when he sinned in that way, or I might have struck him dead. I see that as a VERY serious breach of leadership.

Moses had been up on the mountain for so long that the people gave up on him and turned to other gods. Rather than hold them firmly to their faith in God, Aaron asked the people to give him their gold, and from it he designed an idol. On top of that, when confronted about this unspeakable sin, he lied. He said that he had just thrown the gold into the fire, and the golden calf had jumped out at him. What a terrible untruth!

The fact is that the people were drunken and naked and dancing around that golden calf, totally given to idolatry and lust, and it was all Aaron's fault. If I had been God, I would have punished him severely. Instead, God forgave Aaron and restored him to leadership. Imagine that!

Now, because Moses struck the rock instead of speaking to it as he was commanded to do, he was prevented from entering the Promised Land – and so was Aaron. That's a very heavy penalty. Why would they have incurred such a harsh penalty?

There were a few vaguely similar stories in the Bible, and I thought I had come to understand them. For instance, when I first read the story of David bringing the Ark back into Jerusalem and what happened to Uzzah, I could hardly believe what I was reading. *How could God be so severe?* I wondered, just as David had wondered in his day. Uzzah had only been trying to steady the Ark because the oxen had stumbled. He hadn't done anything wrong. Why should he die for that?

I came to understand that the presence of God which the Ark represented was so sacred and powerful that it could be touched only by those who were authorized to do so. I had to seek God a long while before I finally understood what prevented a man as wonderful as Moses from entering the Promised Land.

It was only in New Testament times that it became apparent who and what the *"rock"* in the wilderness represented:

> *Moreover, brethren, I would not that ye should be ignorant, how that all our fathers were under the cloud, and all passed through the sea; and were all baptized unto Moses in the cloud and in the sea; and did all eat the same spiritual meat; and did all drink the same spiritual drink: for they drank of that spiritual Rock that followed them: and that Rock was Christ.*
>
> *But with many of them God was not well pleased: for they were overthrown in the wilderness. Now these things were our examples, to the intent we should not lust after evil things, as they also lusted.*
>
> 1 Corinthians 10:1-6

"That Rock was Christ!" Wow! The word *smite* used with regard to Moses' action toward the rock means "to give wounds to, to strike, to beat." This explains a lot. Everything the children of Israel experienced in the wilderness was symbolic of the life to come in Jesus. *"That Rock was Christ,"* and it was the striking of it that brought forth the water of life for the people. This would explain why it was such a serious thing to strike it twice.

Moses, who was usually very careful to obey God to the smallest detail, on this occasion made a most serious mistake because he was provoked by the murmuring of the people. As a consequence, he angrily struck the rock. It wasn't necessary, because it had already been struck once, and since it was symbolic of Christ, this simple act became a serious breach of faith and brought a most serious punishment upon this otherwise meek and obedient servant of the Lord.

The Scriptures warn us about *"crucify[ing] the Son of God afresh."* When it is done, we *"put him to an open shame"* (Hebrews 6:6). Is it possible that we are guilty of this same sin? "Oh, I would never do that," most people think, but are we not crucifying the Lord again when we continually beg Him to do what He has already done? Are we not putting Him *"to an open shame"* when we fail to appropriate what His sacrifice has provided for us, or when we continually live below our privileges?

Are you begging the Lord to do what He's already done? Are you continually asking Him to finish what He has already finished? Do you cry out to Him to provide what He has already provided? Then you may be guilty of crucifying Him *"afresh."*

Are you afraid of the devil, when he has already been defeated? Are you asking God for something He has already given to you? It is time to know Jesus in *"the power of His resurrection."* It is time to know what He has already accomplished for us. Until we know the benefits of Calvary and the empty tomb, we will never be successful in the Christian life.

When we come to a difficult place in life, do we murmur as the Israelites did? Why is that? Hasn't God always provided for His people? Was not the water there all along? Is it not a matter of us drinking what He has already provided?

The Rock has already been smitten. The price has already been paid. Salvation is complete. Drink!

Jesus has already been crucified. He carried all of our sins to the cross. He finished the work. And, furthermore, He has already been raised up from the dead, has been glorified, and is even now seated at the right hand of the Father in glory.

Jesus has already defeated the devil, and that is the Good News of the Gospel. Jesus died for sin. He paid the price for the whole world. He suffered so that we might not have to suffer. He died so that we might live. He took all authority away from Satan so that we need not fear him any longer.

What did He do with that authority? He turned around and offered it to us. "Here," He said, "now you can go in My name and use My authority."

Satan is defeated! If that doesn't excite you, then you must be dead. When I hear the Gospel, it ignites a fire within my soul. It fills me with strength and zeal. If it doesn't do something for you, you need to be resurrected.

It is time to stop the complaining. Far too many are saying, "Oh, God, I'm dying here in this wilderness. Why are You not helping me?" That attitude won't get us very far. Stop trying to do everything yourself, and let the Lord do it for you. God said to me, "My people have been trying to be *achievers*, and I want them to be *receivers*." You can't live the victorious life in your own strength. Start depending more on the Lord and on what He has already accomplished for you.

The Lord said, "My people are trying to conquer, when I've already conquered. I just want them to sit with Me in heavenly places and rest in Me. They're trying to excel and prevail, and I just want them to stand strong in what I have given them. They're trying to gain ascendancy, and I just want them to resist the devil."

The Lord didn't say we had to fight the devil. We

have no power to do that. We are just to "resist" him in the power and authority of Jesus.

If we resist him, the promise of God is sure:

> *Submit yourselves therefore to God. Resist the devil, and he will flee from you.*　　　James 4:7

If you can understand what Jesus has done for you, it will put the enemy to flight. Too many are struggling, trying to reach the top. If we can understand what Jesus has done for us, we can rejoice in His victory and walk in it ourselves. We were destined for a state of perpetual thanksgiving.

Too many of us are still struggling to possess what the Lord has already taken possession of for us. We are trying to perform, fighting and struggling to make progress, when all He wants us to do is abide in Him and in the provision He has made, rejoice and live in His divine providence. He has finished the work. It's done. Stop waiting for what is already here. Stop looking for what has already appeared. Receive it and walk in it.

What God did for the children of Israel in the wilderness was glorious:

> *He brought them forth also with silver and gold: and there was not one feeble person among their tribes. Egypt was glad when they departed: for*

the fear of them fell upon them. He spread a cloud for a covering; and fire to give light in the night. The people asked, and he brought quails, and satisfied them with the bread of heaven. He opened the rock, and the waters gushed out; they ran in the dry places like a river.   Psalm 105:37-41

When God *"brought them forth"* (a type of what Jesus has done for us), He did so with style. They were laden down with *"silver and gold."* They also experienced healing and divine health, so that *"there was not one feeble person among their tribes."* The absolutely amazing thing about this statement is that there were anywhere from two to three million or more of these people by then. That's a lot of people to not have even one sick person among them. What a miracle!

Now, why would Egypt be so glad to get rid of these people, especially since, as slaves, the Israelites represented a great source of wealth for Egypt? The reason is that the Egyptians were afraid of the Israelites, and they were afraid of them because it was so apparent that God was with them.

As they came out of Egypt, God's presence continued to be with them. It was seen by day as a cloud, and by night as a fire. That same glory was seen by everyone the day the wilderness Tabernacle was dedicated and the day the Temple in Jerusalem was dedicated. God was with His people, and He wanted everyone to know it.

When the Church was born on the Day of Pentecost, fire fell from Heaven to confirm what God was doing. The same glory that gave light and heat to the Israelites in the wilderness sat upon the disciples that day in Jerusalem.

What more could the Israelites have asked for? God gave them light and heat. He fed them with bread from Heaven and with quail when they were tired of heavenly bread. Then, to top it all off, He *"opened the rock, and the waters gushed out."*

I want to pause and ask you: If the children of Israel could experience all that in the wilderness, what are you worried about? What harm can possibly come to you? What enemy can possibly defeat you? What need can possibly deter you? We have so much more than they had. We are basking in all the benefits of Calvary.

Imagine! Striking that rock was a more grievous and more heavy-duty sin than idolatry. It was worse than making a golden calf and causing other people to worship it. Why was that?

There can be only one explanation. The rock represented Jesus. He has already been struck. He was already smitten for us. He has already been crucified for us. He was buried for us. He rose from the dead for us.

Moses was severely punished because what he did was a prophetic act, and the rock had already been smitten. Striking again implied that what Jesus had already done for us was not sufficient for all time. And nothing could be further from the truth.

We must always remember the terrible consequence of striking the rock again. Jesus must not be *"crucified afresh."* He has already done the work for us. He has already defeated Satan. He doesn't need to do that again. Satan's authority has been taken from him. Jesus paralyzed him, stomped on him and knocked his teeth out.

Don't ever ask Jesus to redo what He's already done. Get to know Him in the power of His resurrection. Get acquainted with what He has already done for you. And, most important of all, start partaking of the benefits.

Part II:

What Jesus Has Done for Us on the Cross

(The Sevenfold Sacrifice of Christ on Calvary)

Chapter Three

What His Sacrifice Means

And the Word was made flesh, and dwelt among us, (and we beheld his glory, the glory as of the only begotten of the Father,) full of grace and truth.
John 1:14

It always amazes me when good Christians, even Spirit-filled Christians, do not know what they have in God. What Jesus accomplished in His death and resurrection opened up to us a whole new and wonderful world.

Recently, I was in a public place, and a seven-year-old girl came over and began to witness to me. Her parents had trained her at home to witness for the Lord, and she was practicing on me.

She was very sweet, and even though she was stumbling over her words, what she was saying was precious. Her most important point was that Jesus had died for us, and I wholeheartedly agreed with her that this is a powerful truth. Oh, how I wish that all believers of whatever age understood the benefits of the death and resurrection of Jesus.

Death and resurrection represent two aspects of Jesus' ministry for us – the past and the present. The fact that He died for us is the past tense aspect of His ministry and the one we want to address in this next section of the book. The fact of His resurrection must not be overlooked, however. Although He died for us, He is now living for us.

The very best illustration I can think of for this truth is what happens to a man and a woman when they decide to marry. They have been leading separate lives until that moment, making their separate plans, doing as they wished. But when they make a commitment to give themselves to one another, their lives dramatically change. They stop living for self and begin living for each other.

Now, they eat the same things, they go to the same places, and when they make plans, it isn't for themselves as individuals. They are planning for two now. They have actually given up their individual lives for the sake of the marriage.

In a much greater and more noble sense, Jesus gave up His life for you and me. There were two parts of that giving. He died for us, and He now lives for us. Jesus is living for us right now. This is a truth that far too many have been blinded to, and it is time to correct that error.

Jesus took on flesh for you and me. That God would

humble Himself because of His love for us is an awesome truth. When the Scriptures say of Jesus that He is *"the same yesterday, and to day, and for ever"* (Hebrews 13:8), they are speaking of Him before He became flesh for us.

There was a short period of time in which He willingly limited Himself and walked the shores of Galilee in the flesh. There was an even shorter period of time in which He chose to suffer in the flesh for our redemption. He died for us on Calvary, He was raised up from the dead, and He is even now sitting at the right hand of the Father in Heaven.

After He had risen from the dead, He was eager to show His disciples that He was flesh:

> *Behold my hands and my feet, that it is I myself: handle me, and see; for a spirit hath not flesh and bones, as ye see me have.* Luke 24:39

He had become flesh for you and me.

All through the Word of God, we see bold statements of truth about why this becoming flesh had to be. For instance:

> *Wherefore in all things it behoved him to be made like unto his brethren, that he might be a merciful and faithful high priest in things pertaining to God, to make reconciliation for the sins of the people.* Hebrews 2:17

Jesus had *"to be made like unto his brethren"* so that
He could become our merciful and faithful High Priest.
He could not be our High Priest without becoming
flesh for us. This act qualified Him. He had to be able
to feel what we feel and to experience what we experience. He had to be tempted as we are tempted. He
had to feel the guilt and pain we bear as a result of
sin.

Jesus knows how it feels to be guilty. He took upon
Himself the chastisement necessary for our peace. He
knows how it feels to experience sickness and disease.
He knows how it feels to experience weakness. He
had to become flesh in order to do all this for us:

> *Forasmuch then as the children are partakers of
> flesh and blood, he also himself likewise took part
> of the same; that through death he might destroy
> him that had the power of death, that is, the devil.*
> Hebrews 2:14

Jesus partook of flesh so that He could destroy *"him
that had the power of death."* He did it to deliver us. He
had to take on flesh to accomplish that.

The fact that *"the Word was made flesh"* has two important meanings. He became flesh to die for us, but
He also can manifest Himself in our flesh, in us. That's
part of the Gospel too. When you receive a miracu-

lous healing, that is the Word being manifested in your flesh. This is God's will for us.

Jesus *"was made in the likeness of men":*

> *But made himself of no reputation, and took upon him the form of a servant, and was made in the likeness of men.* Philippians 2:7

Jesus humbled Himself to take on the likeness of men. In doing so, he conquered Satan and delivered us:

> *And having spoiled principalities and powers, he made a show of them openly, triumphing over them in it.* Colossians 2:15

What did He accomplish?

> *Who hath delivered us from the power of darkness, and hath translated us into the kingdom of his dear Son: in whom we have redemption through his blood, even the forgiveness of sins.* Colossians 1:13-14

It is because of this sacrifice that Jesus has become *"the head of the body, the church":*

> *And he is the head of the body, the church: who is the beginning, the firstborn from the dead; that in*

> *all things he might have the preeminence. For it*
> *pleased the Father that in him should all fulness*
> *dwell.*   Colossians 1:18-19

Jesus' victory made possible our victory. He was the firstfruits, the beginning of this new creation, the firstborn from the dead. It is in Him that we have redemption. If we can get our minds renewed with these truths, it will transform the way we think and act every day.

After we become new creatures in Christ, we have a lot of developing to do, a lot of growing to accomplish. As we renew our minds with the truths of God's Word, we are changed *"from glory to glory"* and begin to take on the likeness of Christ.

We can't change ourselves through our own willpower. We can't change ourselves just because we make a New Year's resolution. We can only change as we understand and know what Jesus has done for us in His death and resurrection.

These resurrection truths may not seem reasonable to many. Indeed, much of the Word of God seems unreasonable to the natural mind. So stop trying to reason things out in your own mind and ask the Holy Spirit to give you a revelation of God's resurrection truths. If you can receive them, your life will be transformed.

Jesus died and was raised again to save us. This little

word *save* carries a very big meaning. It represents all that eternal life holds for the believer.

Jesus came to earth in the flesh, and He suffered on the cross of Calvary. I would not dare to suggest that I understand all that He did there. One day, we will have a heavenly video replay of it, and perhaps we'll understand it all then.

What I do know is that He defeated Satan and took away his authority, and this made possible my escape from the kingdom of darkness and my translation into the Kingdom of God's dear Son. Jesus has been raised up from the dead, and He has all authority.

What Jesus did in Gethsemane and on Golgotha was for us. And the authority he took from Satan, He has given to us and commissioned us to go forth in His name. Let us now explore some of the things Jesus achieved for us on Calvary. I call them The Seven-fold Sacrifice of Christ on Calvary.

Chapter Four

He Died for Us

> *I am crucified with Christ: nevertheless I live; yet not I, but Christ liveth in me: and the life which I now live in the flesh I live by the faith of the Son of God, who loved me, and GAVE HIMSELF FOR ME.* Galatians 2:20

The first resurrection truth we want to consider is that Jesus died for us in every sense of the word. He allowed Himself to be executed on a cross. His blood ran out, and He expired. In that moment, Jesus was totally dead, totally separated from life. He chose to do this. He died so that we might live. He accepted not just physical death, but spiritual death as well, and He did it for you and me. Every man or woman born into this world is destined to die, but Jesus took that death upon Himself so that He could give us the gift of eternal life.

When God placed Adam and Eve in the Garden of

Eden, He warned them not to partake of the tree of the knowledge of good and evil. If they did, He warned, they would *"surely die."* Both Adam and Eve chose to disregard God's warning, and death came upon the entire human race as a result. In His death, Christ paid the price for our disobedience. This is why Paul could say, *"The life which I now live in the flesh I live by the faith of the Son of God, who loved me, and gave himself for me"* (Galatians 2:20).

The result of Adam's sin was that *"death passed upon all men"*:

> *Wherefore, as by one man sin entered into the world, and death by sin; and so death passed upon all men, for that all have sinned.*
>
> Romans 5:12

That includes us. We were as good as dead before Christ gave Himself for us:

> *For ye are dead, and your life is hid with Christ in God.*   Colossians 3:3

Now, we are *"crucified with him"*:

> *Knowing this, that our old man is crucified with him, that the body of sin might be destroyed, that henceforth we should not serve sin.*
>
> Romans 6:6

Likewise reckon ye also yourselves to be dead indeed unto sin, but alive unto God through Jesus Christ our Lord.　　　　Romans 6:11

Why would we believe a contrary report? This is what God has said, and this is what we must believe and declare.

Start getting resurrection truths alive in your heart and in your mouth, and you will begin to talk and act differently. Stop talking weakness, and start talking strength. Stop talking failure, and start talking success. You are crucified with Christ. You should not serve sin. You are dead to sin. Your life is hid with Christ in God.

Let your spirit man be full of these truths. Let your mind be renewed by them, and let them make a difference in you and in everyone around you.

It is not necessary to dwell on sin, and it is time to stop having condemning services in our churches. People don't need to feel condemned; they need to feel lifted up. Christ did not come to condemn, but to deliver men from their sins. Let the Spirit do the convicting of sinners, for He has the power to change the hearts of men.

Remorse alone will not change people. Repentance is more than that. If all we are giving people is a sin consciousness, we're not helping them much. Most sinners already know how weak they are, how dirty they are, how sinful they are. Satan has already told them a thousand times how "no good" they are. They need to hear about the solution. They need to hear that Jesus has paid the price for their sin. Let's not be guilty of bringing death upon sinners. Jesus took our spiritual death upon Himself, and in its place, He gave us eternal life. Share that life with others.

Chapter Five

He Died Unto Sin

> *For in that he died, HE DIED UNTO SIN once: but in that he liveth, he liveth unto God. Likewise reckon ye also yourselves to be dead indeed unto sin, but alive unto God through Jesus Christ our Lord.* Romans 6:10-11

The second resurrection truth we want to consider is that Jesus died unto sin. He took my sins to the cross, and in the place of them, He gave me His righteousness. What a deal! What a great exchange! For my sins, I get the righteousness of Christ.

Righteousness is not something we work for. It is not something we earn by keeping a list of rules and regulations. Righteousness is a gift. It is something that God does on the inside of us. He sovereignly renders us righteous, and that righteousness is not ours. It is His.

The only way we can receive this grace, of course,

is by hearing and believing the Gospel. It is also important, however, to get these truths into our hearts and into our mouths and to begin to confess them before man, before our enemy and before God. We must *"reckon,"* or consider, ourselves dead to sin and alive unto God, through His sacrifice. Jesus has done it for us, so let us receive it and rejoice in it.

This is much more than forgiveness. As we have seen, the people of the Old Testament already had forgiveness. This is redemption through the blood of Jesus. Although the Old Testament saints had forgiveness through the blood of animals, they were not delivered from the effect and the power of sin as we are. God has promised that through the New Covenant, by the blood of Jesus, He would forgive us. But He has also said something utterly amazing: that He would not remember our sins against us anymore.

How is that possible, seeing that our God is all-knowing? He has chosen to block our sins out of His remembrance. What wonderful love and grace! He has so powerfully eradicated our sins that they are gone even from His remembrance. They no longer exist. He has removed them *"as far as the east is from the west"*:

> *As far as the east is from the west, so far hath he removed our transgressions from us.*
> Psalm 103:12

The only place past sins are recorded now is in your mind or in the minds of your friends and loved ones. You can also blot out this record of sins in your mind by hearing the Word of God and getting it into your heart and into your mouth.

Jesus not only forgives us, but He *"cleanse[s] us from all unrighteousness"*:

> *If we confess our sins, he is faithful and just to forgive us our sins, and to cleanse us from all unrighteousness.* 1 John 1:9

That's a lot more than forgiveness, and this righteousness is a free gift.

Not long ago, I saw a documentary about the Orient. A holy man had made a vow that he would remain standing for twelve years to please the gods, and he had already completed seven years of his vow. Can you imagine such a thing? This man had the idea that if he was able to discipline his flesh for years at a time, the gods would be pleased. How sad!

Others crawl on their hands and knees until they are bleeding. They think that if they subject their bodies to these outward afflictions, this will qualify them to approach God. These and all the other acts men do to make themselves worthy to approach God are of no avail. We can only come to Him by grace.

The Gospel is so profound, yet it is amazingly

simple. Jesus died for us. He took our sins on the cross that we might be free of them. That is the Gospel, the Good News of Christ.

Jesus took our spiritual death and gave us His eternal life. He died in our place, as our sacrifice:

Who his own self bare our sins in his own body on the tree, that we, being dead to sins, should live unto righteousness.   1 Peter 2:24

This is the only way righteousness comes. It does not come to us because we do good deeds. It is the gift of God through the sacrifice of Jesus on the cross.

For those who are already believers, this is also an important truth. Righteousness does not come by how many times we go to church (although, when we become righteous, we want to go and give God thanks). Righteousness is a simple work of grace on the inside of you that comes only by what Jesus has done for us in His death and resurrection. He died to sin for me, and I am alive unto God because of it.

Chapter Six

He Died Unto the Law

Wherefore, my brethren, ye also are become DEAD TO THE LAW by the body of Christ; that ye should be married to another, even to him who is raised from the dead, that we should bring forth fruit unto God.   Romans 7:4

For I through the law am DEAD TO THE LAW, that I might live unto God.   Galatians 2:19

The third resurrection truth we want to consider is that Jesus died to the Law for us, and we are now *"dead to the law through the body of Christ."* We see this clearly in Paul's letters to the churches.

In these passages, Paul was talking about the Old Testament Law, the Mosaic Law. Through the sacrifice of Christ, we have been removed from under the old Law, and we have been given a new law, the law of Christ. This new law is faith working by love, and if we keep this new law in Christ Jesus, we will totally satisfy all of God's requirements.

What the Old Testament Law could not do, the law of Christ can accomplish for us:

> *Knowing that a man is not justified by the works of the law, but by the faith of Jesus Christ, even we have believed in Jesus Christ, that we might be justified by the faith of Christ, and not by the works of the law: for by the works of the law shall no flesh be justified.* Galatians 2:16

Paul was not preaching something that he had been taught. It was revealed to him by the Holy Spirit Himself, and this Gospel declares salvation, not through the Law, but through Christ's sacrifice on Calvary.

Christ was the inheritor of the promises given to Abraham, but those promises were not to be realized in the Law. They could only come about through Christ:

> *Now to Abraham and his seed were the promises made. He saith not, And to seeds, as of many; but as of one, And to thy seed, which is Christ. And this I say, that the covenant, that was confirmed before of God in Christ, the law, which was four hundred and thirty years after, cannot disannul, that it should make the promise of none effect. For*

if the inheritance be of the law, it is no more of
promise: but God gave it to Abraham by promise.
                              Galatians 3:16-18

Even Abraham had to believe, and we have a new
law of faith working by love. This is confirmed by
many other scriptures. For instance, Paul warned the
Galatians not to go back to the old Law for salvation,
calling it *"the yoke of bondage"*:

> *Stand fast therefore in the liberty wherewith Christ*
> *hath made us free, and be not entangled again*
> *with the yoke of bondage.*   Galatians 5:1

> *For in Jesus Christ neither circumcision availeth*
> *any thing, nor uncircumcision; but faith which*
> *worketh by love.*   Galatians 5:6

This, then, is the New Testament law, faith working
by love.

I'm so glad that God has given us a better way. If
our New Covenant was dependent on an outward law
of rules and regulations like the Ten Commandments,
we would fail, just as those who endeavored to keep
the old Law. This Law was changed because it was
"weak through the flesh":

> *For what the law could not do, in that it was*
> *weak through the flesh, God sending his own Son*

*in the likeness of sinful flesh, and for sin, con-
demned sin in the flesh.*   Romans 8:3

The flesh is never strong enough, and our willpower is never strong enough to keep rules and regulations. This righteousness that we have is a gift. This new life, this eternal life that we have is a free gift of God. It is the righteousness of God in Jesus Christ.

Many people stumble over this truth. The Gospel seems much too simple to suit them. That's sad, because God has simplified it on purpose, so that you and I would have the hope of salvation.

Our salvation rests in what Jesus has done for us, and our victory rests in knowing Him in the power of His resurrection.

Chapter Seven

He Died Unto the Curse

Christ hath redeemed us from the curse of the law, BEING MADE A CURSE FOR US: for it is written, Cursed is every one that hangeth on a tree: that the blessing of Abraham might come on the Gentiles through Jesus Christ; that we might receive the promise of the Spirit through faith.
Galatians 3:13-14

The fourth resurrection truth we want to consider is that Jesus died unto the curse of that Old Testament Law, and in place of the curse He has given us His blessings. This is what He meant by *"the blessing of Abraham."*

We are redeemed from the curse. And what was this curse? The curse defined in the Old Testament included being given into the hand of one's enemies. It included suffering sickness and disease. It included suffering crop failure. It included seeing one's children taken into bondage. We don't want any of those things. We want *"the blessing of Abraham,"* and it can come upon us only *"through Jesus Christ."*

What Paul referred to as *"the promise of the Spirit"* could mean one of two things. It could refer to the gift of the Holy Spirit, or it could refer to the promises the Holy Spirit made to us in the Scriptures.

The Scriptures very clearly define blessings upon those who love and serve God and curses upon those who deny Him. One of the most powerful passages in this regard begins as follows:

> *Behold, I set before you this day a blessing and a curse; a blessing, if ye obey the commandments of the LORD your God, which I command you this day: and a curse, if ye will not obey the commandments of the LORD your God, but turn aside out of the way which I command you this day, to go after other gods, which ye have not known.*
>
> Deuteronomy 11:26-28

Another section of Deuteronomy spells out very clearly the blessings and the curses (see chapter 28). One of the blessings promised was: becoming *"the head, and not the tail,"* to *"be above only, and ... not be beneath"* (verse 13). Other verses in that chapter show that we are to be blessed in everything that we set our hand to. We are to prosper, and our enemies are to flee from us. What wonderful promises!

When the woes of Revelation are spoken, we can know that those of us who are in Christ Jesus are not included. While the world is experiencing woes, we will be rejoicing in the Lord. Our curse was placed upon Jesus, and He has given us His blessings in its place.

Chapter Eight

He Died Unto the Flesh

> *And you hath he quickened, who were dead in tres-*
> *passes and sins; wherein in time past ye walked*
> *according to the course of this world, according to*
> *the prince of the power of the air, the spirit that*
> *now worketh in the children of disobedience: among*
> *whom also we all had our conversation in times*
> *past in the lusts of our flesh, fulfilling the desires of*
> *the flesh and of the mind; and were by nature the*
> *children of wrath, even as others.*
>
> Ephesians 2:1-3

The fifth resurrection truth we want to consider is that Jesus died unto the flesh. He became flesh so that He could take our flesh to the cross. In exchange, He has given us the true circumcision of the heart. What does this mean for us?

We understand and know, as we read the Gospel, that before we came to Christ, we were controlled by the flesh, and that is bad news. Paul, for instance, detailed *"the works of the flesh"*:

> *Now the works of the flesh are manifest, which are these; Adultery, fornication, uncleanness, lasciviousness, idolatry, witchcraft, hatred, variance, emulations, wrath, strife, seditions, heresies, envyings, murders, drunkenness, revellings, and such like: of the which I tell you before, as I have also told you in time past, that they which do such things shall not inherit the kingdom of God.*
> Galatians 5:19-21

Before we were born again, we were actually controlled by *"the prince of the power of the air,"* and our conduct revealed that fact. We *"were by nature the children of wrath."* But, those of us who *"are Christ's"* have received a wonderful miracle:

> *And they that are Christ's have crucified the flesh with the affections and lusts.*   Galatians 5:24

This wonderful crucifixion of the flesh has become possible only *"through Christ Jesus"*:

> *But God, who is rich in mercy, for his great love wherewith he loved us, even when we were dead in sins, hath quickened us together with Christ, (by grace ye are saved;) and hath raised us up together,*

and made us sit together in heavenly places in Christ Jesus: that in the ages to come he might show the exceeding riches of his grace in his kindness toward us through Christ Jesus. Ephesians 2:4-7

The Old Testament provided for circumcision, which was symbolic of the cleansing of the flesh. But real circumcision, that *"of the heart,"* could come about only through Jesus and His sacrifice for us:

For he is not a Jew, which is one outwardly; neither is that circumcision, which is outward in the flesh: but he is a Jew, which is one inwardly; and circumcision is that of the heart, in the spirit, and not in the letter; whose praise is not of men, but of God. Romans 2:28-29

Through Christ, a miracle was performed on us, and we have been purged of flesh. This means that the control the flesh once exercised over us has been severed, just as Paul taught the Colossians:

In whom also ye are circumcised with the circumcision made without hands, in putting off the body of the sins of the flesh by the circumcision of Christ: buried with him in baptism, wherein also ye are risen with him through the faith of the operation of God, who hath raised him from the dead.
Colossians 2:11

This circumcision of the heart is an actual operation, a literal surgical procedure. This is a divine intervention. God actually cuts out the old and implants the new in us. The Amplified Bible renders this verse thus:

> *In Him also you were circumcised with a circumcision not made with hands, but in a [spiritual] circumcision [performed by] Christ by stripping off the body of the flesh (the whole corrupt, carnal nature with its passions and lusts.)*
>
> Colossians 2:11, AMP

This is why we can say that we are *"dead with Christ"* (Colossians 2:20). We have died to the world's way of thinking and acting. And, if we are dead with Christ, we are also *"risen with Him"*:

> *Buried with him in baptism, wherein also ye are risen with him through the faith of the operation of God, who hath raised him from the dead.*
>
> Colossians 2:12

This enables us to *"set [our] affection on things above"*:

> *Set your affection on things above, not on things on the earth. For ye are dead, and your life is hid with Christ in God.*   Colossians 3:2-3

We, therefore, have become *"the circumcision":*

For we are the circumcision, which worship God in the spirit, and rejoice in Christ Jesus, and have no confidence in the flesh.   Philippians 3:3

When we have a revelation of what Jesus has done for us in His death and resurrection, we are able to begin to concentrate on heavenly things, and this is important. Whatever gets our attention will also receive our affection. If we can set our affection on things above, if we can continually think on these resurrection truths and keep them in our hearts and minds, we will be overcomers.

John wrote very forcefully to the members of the early Church:

Love not the world, neither the things that are in the world. If any man love the world, the love of the Father is not in him. For all that is in the world, the lust of the flesh, and the lust of the eyes, and the pride of life, is not of the Father, but is of the world. And the world passeth away, and the lust thereof: but he that doeth the will of God abideth for ever.   1 John 2:15-17

We have a covenant of prosperity. It is not wrong to have money or the things it buys, but if we begin to love this world, it will dominate our affection. As the Scriptures so clearly show:

> *For the love of money is the root of all evil: which while some coveted after, they have erred from the faith, and pierced themselves through with many sorrows.* 1 Timothy 6:10

God's blessings must never become a curse to us by replacing Him in our devotion. The flesh that had control over us has been cut:

> *Therefore consider the members of your earthly body as dead to immorality, impurity, passion, evil desire, and greed, which amounts to idolatry.*
> Colossians 3:5, NAS

> *Likewise reckon ye also yourselves to be dead indeed unto sin, but alive unto God through Jesus Christ our Lord. Let not sin therefore reign in your mortal body, that ye should obey it in the lusts thereof. Neither yield ye your members as instruments of unrighteousness unto sin: but yield yourselves unto God, as those that are alive from the dead, and your members as instruments of righteousness unto God.* Romans 6:11-13

Get past the devil. Stop wrestling with him in your mind. He wants you to think you are too weak to prevail, that you have committed too many sins in the past to survive. He is a liar. Know what Jesus has done for you. You are freed from the flesh through Christ.

This wonderful circumcision of the heart was foretold in Old Testament times:

> *And the LORD thy God will circumcise thine heart, and the heart of thy seed, to love the LORD thy God with all thine heart, and with all thy soul, that thou mayest live.*   Deuteronomy 30:6

This denying of the flesh is not something you can do on your own, some *"self-abasement and severe treatment of the body"*:

> *These are matters which have, to be sure, the appearance of wisdom in self-made religion and self-abasement and severe treatment of the body, but are of no value against fleshly indulgence.*
> Colossians 2:23, NAS

Holy living is not just neglecting certain things. It is the putting off of the flesh through the sacrifice of Christ. This can only be accomplished through a revelation of what He has done for us through His death and resurrection.

Chapter Nine

He Died Unto Sickness and Disease

Who his own self bare our sins in his own body on the tree, that we, being dead to sins, should live unto righteousness: BY WHOSE STRIPES YE WERE HEALED.   1 Peter 2:24

The sixth resurrection truth we want to consider is that Jesus died unto sickness and disease. He carried our physical sufferings on Himself to the cross, and in their place, He now offers us healing and divine health. Healing is wonderful, but divine health is even better, and they are both ours through Christ.

Some Christians are already walking in this truth, but this is where God wants us all to be. There is no reason for you to live in condemnation if you haven't yet been able to receive healing or divine health, but at least know that it is available to you. God is no respecter of persons. He does not offer healing to one and not to another.

This is not a difficult teaching to receive. None of God's ways are difficult. The Bible is not so far over our heads that we can never reach it, as some people seem to think.

Healing does not depend on finding the right person to pray for you. If you will just touch the hem of the Master's garment, you will be healed, and you can even do that without anyone else helping you. Receiving healing is easy, so if we don't have it yet, it's not God's fault.

This is one of the bold and vital resurrection facts of the Bible, and whether we understand it or not, whether we have experienced it or not, whether we have heard others testify to it or not, that doesn't change it. Jesus died for our sicknesses and diseases, and He has given us health and healing. It's that simple.

The prophet Isaiah gave us a very graphic description of Jesus dying on the cross for us and what He suffered there:

> *He is despised and rejected of men; a man of sorrows, and acquainted with grief: and we hid as it were our faces from him; he was despised, and we esteemed him not. Surely he hath borne our griefs, and carried our sorrows: yet we did esteem him stricken, smitten of God, and afflicted. But he was*

> *wounded for our transgressions, he was bruised*
> *for our iniquities: the chastisement of our peace*
> *was upon him; and with his stripes we are healed.*
>   Isaiah 53:3-5

Before His death, Jesus was turned over to a large band of soldiers who mocked Him and made sport of Him, beating Him, pulling out His hair and spitting on Him. Can you imagine the precious Son of God covered with the spittle of those men? Can you imagine the Son of God with His beard pulled out by the roots?

The whip they used to beat Jesus was made up of many separate thongs, and onto the end of each one of those thongs a sharp piece of metal was fastened. Each time they lashed Jesus, those pieces of metal ripped His skin open and tore away more flesh. His body was so brutally beaten that He no longer resembled a man. His flesh must have literally looked like hamburger meat.

Now, why would Jesus have gone through all that? He didn't need to defeat the devil for Himself. He was God. He had nothing to prove. All of this suffering was for us. Jesus didn't need to die; He did it for us.

Jesus' sufferings on the cross were not all physical. He bore *"our griefs, and carried our sorrows."* As we have seen, He knows how it feels to be guilty of the most vile sin, because He tasted of that guilt. He took upon Himself the chastisement, the punishment, necessary for our peace. He took upon Himself our weaknesses. He took our pains, our sorrows, our sicknesses and our diseases.

What an awesome truth! To me, there is nothing worse than guilt. I hate to feel guilty, because I'm very sensitive to it. I thank God that Jesus took my guilt. He was my substitute. He bore my punishment. He made the choice of dividing *"the spoils"* of His victory with us:

> *Therefore will I divide him a portion with the great, and he shall divide the spoil with the strong; because he hath poured out his soul unto death: and he was numbered with the transgressors; and he bare the sin of many, and made intercession for the transgressors.* Isaiah 53:12

We have nothing to take credit for; He has done it all. Our victory is not in how well we can pray or how great our supposed accomplishments are. We are victorious only because He has conquered. A true understanding of the Gospel is humbling. It makes you want to fall at the feet of the Savior and rejoice. He bore in His own flesh both our sins and our sicknesses.

Matthew recorded that the healing miracles Jesus did were in fulfillment of the prophecy of Isaiah:

> *When the even was come, they brought unto him*
> *many that were possessed with devils: and he cast*
> *out the spirits with his word, and healed all that*
> *were sick: that it might be fulfilled which was*
> *spoken by Esaias the prophet, saying, Himself took*
> *our infirmities, and bare our sicknesses.*
>
> Matthew 8:16-17

This declaration of Peter that *"with his stripes we are healed"* ranks right up there on the amazement scale with *"a virgin shall conceive and bear a son"* (Isaiah 7:14). We can't understand intellectually how this is possible. We can't figure it out with our natural minds. In the same way, we may never intellectually comprehend the fact that Jesus died unto sickness and disease for us. But if we believe it in our hearts and get it into our mouths, it will set us free.

Chapter Ten

He Died Unto the World

---

*But God forbid that I should glory, save in the
cross of our Lord Jesus Christ, BY WHOM THE
WORLD IS CRUCIFIED UNTO ME, AND I
UNTO THE WORLD.* Galatians 6:14

The seventh resurrection truth we want to consider
is that Jesus died unto the world for us. Through His
death and resurrection, He has delivered us from the
influence of the world, and instead has hidden us in
Christ Jesus. We have been made to sit with Him in
heavenly places. What an awesome and wonderful
Gospel truth!

When we understand these truths and we believe
them in our hearts, the devil can no longer harass us.
We no longer have to struggle, either with our past
lives or with present temptations.

Some Christians live their entire lives in a struggle
with temptation, a struggle with the devil, the world,

the flesh. This is clearly not the will of God. We can overcome by believing the simple message of the Gospel:

> *If ye then be risen with Christ, seek those things which are above, where Christ sitteth on the right hand of God. Set your affection on things above, not on things on the earth. For ye are dead, and your life is hid with Christ in God.*
>
> Colossians 3:1-3

> *Who gave himself for our sins, that he might deliver us from this present evil world, according to the will of God and our Father.*
>
> Galatians 1:4

> *But God, who is rich in mercy, for his great love wherewith he loved us, even when we were dead in sins, hath quickened us together with Christ, (by grace ye are saved;) and hath raised us up together, and made us sit together in heavenly places in Christ Jesus.* Ephesians 2:4-6

> *Wherefore if ye be dead with Christ, from the rudiments of the world, why, as though living in the world, are ye subject to ordinances?*
>
> Colossians 2:20

He Died Unto the World

Because he hath set his love upon me, therefore will I deliver him: I will set him on high, because he hath known my name.　　Psalm 91:14

What great promises! The price has been paid. All we must do is receive it and act on it. Our Lord Jesus Christ, through His sacrifice, has *"set [us] on high,"* far above the devil and this world.

Part III:

What Jesus Is Doing for Us Now

(The Sevenfold Ministry of Jesus, Our High Priest)

Chapter Eleven

Jesus' Ministry Now

*For if, when we were enemies, we were reconciled
to God by the death of his Son, much more, being
reconciled, we shall be saved BY HIS LIFE.*

Romans 5:10

It is wonderful to understand what the Lord Jesus
has done for us in the past, but it is just as important
to know what He is doing for us NOW. I personally
believe that not many Christians have this revelation.
Most of us realize that Jesus died for us (even if we
don't understand all that this means), but there is a
greater truth. He is living for us NOW, as our current
and actual High Priest.

What an awesome reality! There is much more for
us than just being *"reconciled ... by the death of [God's]
Son."* We can also be *"saved by His life."* Jesus is living
for us right now, today. He still has this ministry. He
didn't just die for us and go off and leave us. If He

had done that, we might have had forgiveness of sins, but left there, forgiven and cleansed of sins but no more, we still could not have lived the victorious Christian life.

Jesus has not left us. He still has a ministry today, and it is operating on our behalf. He is living for us now in the twenty-first century.

Many of the New Testament truths concerning Jesus' ministry as High Priest are contained in the letter to the Hebrews. This is logical, because it was the Hebrews, the Jewish people, who had the high priests of the Old Testament. These high priests were types and shadows of our heavenly High Priest, Jesus.

Many books have been written and countless teachings have been given in churches all over the world about certain aspects of the Old Testament and their relationship to us as believers – the Tabernacle, for instance, and its furniture and symbolic ceremony. Little, however, has been taught or written on Jesus as High Priest now. This is a tragedy! We must not miss what our Lord is offering us in His present capacity. His ministry is not only past; it is present as well. How can we not receive it?

Once we understand that Jesus is our High Priest NOW, we can go back to the Old Testament and learn more about what high priests did then and know what it is that He is doing for us now. As we read the Old Testament, we can see Jesus on every page.

There are also some awesome statements in the book of Hebrews, some bold resurrection facts, that you and I must accept by faith and begin acting upon. You will never mentally or intellectually understand them. You will never reason them out in your mind. Just believe them and begin to put them to work in your daily life.

The Gospel is not reasonable. Nothing about it is reasonable. Nothing about the ways of God is reasonable. Just believe God's bold resurrection truths in your heart and let them change your thinking. Then, get these truths into your mouth and begin to confess them.

For instance:

> *Wherefore he is able also to save them to the uttermost that come unto God by him, seeing he ever liveth to make intercession for them.*
> Hebrews 7:25

What an all-inclusive and absolute truth! In the day in which we live, intellectuals are telling us that there are no absolutes in life. Nothing, however, could be more absolute than the promises of God's Word. His Word is the ultimate absolute.

Jesus, our High Priest, is able to save us absolutely, or *"to the uttermost,"* and He can do that because He is living for us now. This wonderful plan that our Lord has for us, this new life He offers us, is fail-proof. It doesn't have any weaknesses. The Old Covenant was weak, but this covenant is not. It cannot fail, because Jesus is its Guarantor.

Jesus did not do away with the Old Testament Law; He superceded it. There was nothing wrong with the commandments God gave in those times, and they are still valid today. The problem with the Old Testament lay not in the laws themselves, but in the fact that the men who tried to live them were so flawed. They had to depend on their own strength and their own efforts, the works of their flesh. That's why they failed, not because the laws were bad.

Now, however, we have been given a new law, the law of Jesus Christ. This new law cannot fail, because Christ cannot fail and because He is living and working on our behalf.

The old Law was completed, or fulfilled, in Jesus, and now we have a new law. The basis of this new law is Jesus and His role as our High Priest. He is the Author and Finisher of our faith. He is not only our Savior; He is our Mediator and our Intercessor.

These are all legal, or courtroom, terms. Jesus is our Advocate. Just as an earthly courtroom has a judge and jury, a prosecutor and a defense attorney, Jesus is our Advocate. He is the Apostle and the King. The book of Hebrews calls Him Lord, but it also calls Him a sin offering. It shows us that He is so much better than anything found in the Old Testament. This covenant that we have through Him is a *"better covenant"* based upon *"better promises"*:

> *But now hath he obtained a more excellent ministry, by how much also he is the mediator of a better covenant, which was established upon better promises.* Hebrews 8:6

The Old Testament Mercy Seat was wonderful, but now we have something so much better. The prophets of the Old Testament were wonderful, but we have a Prophet who is much better. The angels seen in the Old Testament were wonderful, but we have someone much better than the angels. Jesus is better than Moses, better than Aaron, better than Joshua and better than Melchisedek.

The sacrifices of the Old Testament were wonderful, but we have a much better sacrifice. The ministry of the Old Testament was wonderful, but we have something that cannot be compared. The Tabernacle in the wilderness was wonderful, but we have a better Tabernacle in Heaven. Our New Covenant through Christ far surpasses the Old in every sense of the word.

Through Jesus, we now have access to the Most Holy Place. Under the Old Covenant, only the high priests could enter the Holy of Holies, and they could only go there once a year. Even then, they had to tread carefully or they could be struck dead by the awe-some presence of God. Now, because of what Jesus has done for us (and is doing for us), we can have confidence and boldness to enter the Holiest Place by His blood – anytime and for anything we need. What an awesome truth!

> *And almost all things are by the law purged with blood; and without shedding of blood is no remis-sion. It was therefore necessary that the patterns of things in the heavens should be purified with these; but the heavenly things themselves with better sacrifices than these. For Christ is not entered into the holy places made with hands, which are the figures of the true; but into heaven itself, now to appear in the presence of God for us: nor yet that he should offer himself often, as the high priest entereth into the holy place every year with blood of others; for then must he often have suffered since the foundation of the world: but now once in the end of the world hath he appeared to put away sin by the sacrifice of himself.*

> Hebrews 9:22-26

This has given us the boldness necessary to enter the Holy Place:

> *Having therefore, brethren, boldness to enter into the holiest by the blood of Jesus, by a new and*

living way, which he hath consecrated for us, through the veil, that is to say, his flesh; and having an high priest over the house of God; let us draw near with a true heart in full assurance of faith, having our hearts sprinkled from an evil conscience, and our bodies washed with pure water.
Hebrews 10:19-22

There is such a great depth to our blood covenant with Christ that we could write books about it every week and never exhaust the truths it holds.

In this New Covenant, we are promised a union with God and a communion with Him. Isn't that what we are all seeking? There is a God hunger in each of us to have such a union and a communion with Him, and it is possible through His sacrifice.

Jesus, our High Priest, is available to us. When a man and woman have been married for many years, they form a bond that is unique. They are always there for one another, and it is wonderful to behold. At some point in their long history together, they ceased to make their individual plans. From then on, it was always "we." To a much higher degree, Jesus has made Himself available to us. He is living for us in active ministry.

Now that we understand that Jesus is living for us now, we want to look more closely at seven particular things He is doing for us as our High Priest.

Chapter Twelve

He Is Living to Strengthen Us in Our Time of Temptation

> *Wherefore in all things it behoved him to be made like unto his brethren, that he might be a merciful and faithful high priest in things pertaining to God, to make reconciliation for the sins of the people. For in that he himself hath suffered being tempted, HE IS ABLE TO SUCCOUR THEM THAT ARE TEMPTED.* Hebrews 2:17-18

The first thing that Jesus is doing as our High Priest is living to help us in the time of our need, living to strengthen us in our time of temptation. One day we will receive new and glorified bodies, and the order of life in that day will be much different than it is today. While we are still here on earth and still in our mortal bodies, we desperately need the Lord's help.

The meaning of this King James word *succour* is

"come to the aid of, relieve, help, run to the cry of, or assist." That's what our Lord is able to do for us, because He has already experienced temptation Himself and overcome it.

One of the most important prayers we can ever pray is: *"Help, Lord"* (Psalm 12:1). One prayer that might be considered higher is "Holy! Holy! Holy!" but the reality is that sometimes the only words we have are "Help! Help! Help!" I want to tell you that Jesus understands that kind of prayer. He is living to strengthen us in our time of need, and is ready to help us when we call.

He has said in His Word:

> *For we have not an high priest which cannot be touched with the feeling of our infirmities; but was in all points tempted like as we are, yet without sin. Let us therefore come boldly unto the throne of grace, that we may obtain mercy, and find grace to help in time of need.*   Hebrews 4:15-16

This includes any situation of pressure and any moment of discouragement.

Like each of you, I have been through many difficult situations. I have been through hard places. I call these "places of pressure" or "places of adversity and affliction." During the times I have been experiencing these trials of life, I have sometimes felt, *Lord, is anybody praying for me at all?* I'm sure you know what I am saying. Our flesh can get distracted and become overwhelmed. It happens to all of us at times.

I put a message on my answering machine. It said, "Every time you call on God, He will answer. *We* are not available for your call right now, but *Jesus* is always available. He's always living to strengthen you." We all need to hear this message from time to time. In any kind of adversity and affliction, Jesus is there. He is living for us now.

When we are facing pressure situations in our lives, there is a supernatural work that God does on the inside of us. You may feel discouraged or, as the Scriptures say, *"weary in well doing"* (Galatians 6:9), and when it happens, suddenly you feel that you have no strength, and you're not sure if you can go on. If you can come to Jesus, your High Priest, in moments like this, and pray, "Lord, You're living to strengthen me and to help me," something will begin to change. Then, begin to worship Him. Praise Him, and let His wonderful resurrection truths take hold within you. Start thanking Him for what His Word has promised.

If you can do this, you will suddenly feel something changing on the inside of you. You will suddenly feel hope. You will suddenly feel encouraged. You will suddenly feel strong. It will happen because Jesus is living to strengthen you.

There have been times in my own life when I was feeling so discouraged and weak as I went into prayer that I just wanted to lie down and die. I mean that literally. That's how I felt. But when I got through praying, I would find myself running through the house and jumping on the furniture.

What happened? None of the circumstances that discouraged me and made me want to die had changed, but something had changed on the inside of me. The circumstances were still the same, and there was evidence of a great need in my life, but despite that evidence in the natural, I knew that something had changed. Supernatural strength had poured into me, and I was different.

How was it possible that I was so down one moment and so up the next? It was because Jesus is living for us NOW. Circumstances may not change, but His strength in us changes everything. The throne of grace infuses us with new power when we feel weak.

God's grace is available to us anytime, anywhere and for any need that we have. He is the strength of our lives, and His strength is like none other.

It is not necessary for us to go through this life with a long face, being overcome with circumstances. Jesus is living for us to strengthen us. The enemy of our souls cannot penetrate the presence of God, His glory, on us. I love the psalm that says:

Therefore will not we fear, though the earth be removed, and though the mountains be carried into the midst of the sea. Psalm 46:2

No matter what circumstances you may be facing in the natural, you have someone who is living at the right hand of the Father for you. You can come boldly to Him for any need, anytime and anywhere. He's living to strengthen you.

Strength doesn't come from your intellect. It doesn't come from your mind. It doesn't come from your reasoning power (although we can and should strengthen one another). If you do go to flesh-and-blood people and receive strength from them or through them, it still has to originate with Jesus. There's a place in God that you can come to know Him in such a way that you can run to Him in your time of need, and He will rescue you.

I'm not saying that we don't need other people. We do need each other. But Jesus is the source of all our strength, and He is living for us to strengthen us.

Chapter Thirteen

He Is Living to Execute the Word
We Believe and Confess

> *Wherefore, holy brethren, partakers of the heavenly calling, consider the Apostle and High Priest of our profession, Christ Jesus.*   Hebrews 3:1

The second thing that Jesus, our High Priest, is living to do is to execute the word we believe and confess. He is *"the High Priest of our profession."* The more modern versions of the Bible translate this phrase as *"the High Priest of our CONFESSION."* In recent years, we have been learning just how powerful our words are, but they are powerful only because our High Priest is present to back them up and see that they are executed, or carried out.

What does it mean to *execute*? This is a legal term meaning "to carry out, or enforce." We have officials who execute our existing laws. They do not make laws themselves, but they enforce the laws that have already been passed. Jesus is the Executor, the Enforcer, and He carries out His Word, even when we are the ones declaring it, or confessing it.

Jesus is not working now to defeat Satan. He's already done that. Now He is living to execute the word that we believe and declare. In this respect, He is limited in what He can do for us. This idea might shock some people, and they might ask if I really mean that Jesus can be limited. I do. He can only work for us as we believe. He can only execute for us what we declare to be true – what we confess.

As Christians, we love the Bible, and every word of it is powerful. God has spoken every phrase of it. What God has spoken, however, will not benefit us unless, and until, we get it into our hearts and then speak it with our mouths.

Many people have tripped over this matter of the importance of our confession. They insist:

> *For the word of God is quick [alive], and powerful, and sharper than any twoedged sword, piercing even to the dividing asunder of soul and spirit, and of the joints and marrow, and is a discerner of the thoughts and intents of the heart.*
>
> Hebrews 4:12

While it is true that the Word of God is *"alive and*

powerful," the Holy Spirit has chosen to limit Himself to what we believe and confess. He does not force His blessing upon us. If we will dare to believe what He has spoken and declare it, He will enforce it.

Hebrews again makes this connection between the responsibility of the High Priest and our *"profession"* (confession):

> *And having an high priest over the house of God; let us draw near with a true heart in full assurance of faith ... . Let us hold fast the profession of our faith without wavering (for he is faithful that promised).* Hebrews 10:21-23

There are many scriptural passages that support this truth. To me, one of the best is found in the psalms, when it speaks of the honor we have, to steal from the enemy. It says:

> *Let the high praises of God be in their mouth, and a twoedged sword in their hand; to execute vengeance upon the heathen, and punishments upon the people; to bind their kings with chains, and their nobles with fetters of iron; to execute upon them the judgment written: this honour have all his saints. Praise ye the LORD.*
> Psalm 149:6-9

"The high praises of God" must be in our mouths, and *"a twoedged sword"* must be in our hands. What does this depict? It shows us holding God's Word up to Him and praising Him for it. In this way, we are able to *"execute vengeance upon the heathen, and punishments upon the people."*

The Word of God is not just for reading or hearing. It must go into our hearts; it must be allowed to renew our minds; and it must be found in our mouths. When it is, Jesus will execute it. He will bring it to pass.

Let's say, for instance, that the symptoms of some sickness try to come upon me. The natural thing to do would be to feel sorry for myself and to get on the phone and see how many people I could find who would feel sorry for me and have pity on me. When we're sick, we often feel the need for pity and attention, and I'm sure the devil rejoiced when the telephone was invented.

I used to be guilty of seeking the pity of others for my need. When I got into a pressure place, a hard place, the first thing I did was find someone who would feel sorry for me and agree with me in my distress. The Proverbs show us that this is how we get into trouble (with our words):

> *Thou art snared with the words of thy mouth, thou art taken with the words of thy mouth.*
>
> Proverbs 6:2

That's one alternative, but it's the wrong one. The correct thing to do is to obey Psalm 149 and start praising God. When, in faith, we hold His Word up as our ideal and we begin to thank Him for the fulfillment of His promises, His hand is moved, and He executes that word on our behalf. It works.

Years ago, I was praying one day, attempting to receive healing from the Lord. I was saying all the right things, but it wasn't really coming from my heart. I was moaning and groaning as I declared, "Oh God, I thank You that with Jesus' stripes I was healed."

My husband came to the door of the room where I was praying and said, "I don't know how you sound to God, but you surely are getting on my nerves."

What a learning experience that was for me! I began to think, *I wonder how my prayer sounds to God?*, and thinking about that caused me to brighten up and begin to do what Psalm 149 teaches. I had to let the praises of God be in my mouth, and that soon brought the desired result.

In Numbers, we find this powerful statement of truth:

> *As truly as I live, saith the LORD, as ye have spoken in mine ears, so will I do to you.*
> Numbers 14:28

I believe it, I confess it, and Jesus enforces it.

I have heard some people say: "You have what you say – when you're under the anointing." That is a half-truth. It is true that we have what we say when we're under the anointing, but too many people think that's the only time we can have what we say. This principle is true all the time, even for the nonbelievers and their non-faith words.

Jesus Himself said it:

> *A good man out of the good treasure of his heart bringeth forth that which is good; and an evil man out of the evil treasure of his heart bringeth forth that which is evil: for of the abundance of the heart his mouth speaketh.* Luke 6:45

A good man speaks good things, and what he speaks brings forth good. An evil man speaks evil things, and his evil speech produces evil.

Years ago, when I was teaching this, someone said to me, "That sounds like bondage to me; I don't want to get into that. If I thought I had to be watching every word that came out of my mouth, I would be very uncomfortable. That's not the way I want to live."

But this is not bondage any more than the law of sowing and reaping is bondage. God gave this concept to us for our blessing, not as an additional burden. It is true that this principle could work against you if you didn't understand it and, therefore, you were not careful about this matter. But it was given for life, not for death. It was given that we might increase, that we might be fruitful.

That person said to me, "What if I don't really believe it in my heart? Should I still speak it?" Absolutely! That's the best way to get it into your heart:

> *The words of a man's mouth are as deep waters,*
> *and the wellspring of wisdom as a flowing brook.*
> Proverbs 18:4

> *A man's belly shall be satisfied with the fruit of*
> *his mouth; and with the increase of his lips shall*
> *he be filled. Death and life are in the power of the*
> *tongue: and they that love it shall eat the fruit*
> *thereof.* Proverbs 18:20-21

The more you keep God's words in your mouth, the more they will get inside of you.

It is wrong to think one thing and say something else. If the devil is trying to play on your thoughts, the best thing to do is to speak God's Word – whether you think you believe it or not. If you say it with your mouth, that's the best way to get it on the inside of you. As you believe it and declare it, Jesus, our High Priest, will perform it.

Chapter Fourteen

He Is Living to Make Intercession for Us

My little children, these things write I unto you, that you sin not. And if any man sin, WE HAVE AN ADVOCATE WITH THE FATHER, Jesus Christ the righteous: and he is the propitiation for our sins: and not for ours only, but also for the sins of the whole world. 1 John 2:1-2

The third thing that Jesus, our High Priest, is doing for us right now is living to make intercession for us. Intercession is another courtroom term. An intercessor is a lawyer, an advocate. An intercessor pleads the cause of someone in court. *Intercede* also has the meaning "to pray for, to defend, or to furnish assistance." What an awesome truth! Jesus is our Intercessor!

Sometimes we think nobody is praying for us, and

we get into a self-pitying mood. But I want you to know that Jesus is living to assist you the moment you have a need. He is your lawyer, your Advocate, in the courtroom in Heaven. He can save you *"to the uttermost"*:

> *But this man, because he continueth ever, hath an unchangeable priesthood. Wherefore he is able also to save them to the uttermost that come unto God by him, seeing he ever liveth to make intercession for them. For such an high priest became us, who is holy, harmless, undefiled, separate from sinners, and made higher than the heavens.*
>
> Hebrews 7:24-26

"To the uttermost" represents perfection, or complete- ness. Because Jesus is living for us, He can save us completely. That's about as absolute as you can get.

This is one of those resurrection truths, one of those bold statements of truth, that you can never reason out, just like you'll never reason out how a virgin could conceive and bear a son. It makes no sense to the natural mind that Jesus can take away our sin, but He does it — *"to the uttermost."*

Because He is living for us, our High Priest is able to save us finally and completely. This is why we have a failure-proof covenant. There is no weakness through the flesh in this New Covenant. It doesn't depend on our own strength or our own fleshly efforts. It doesn't depend on how intelligent we are, how educated we are, or how many good works we have done. It depends on Jesus living for us, and He never changes.

There, in the courtroom of Heaven, He is praying for us. He is working for us. He is living for us. He is our Chief Intercessor. How wonderful!

Chapter Fifteen

He Is Living to Administer the Blood Covenant

Neither by the blood of goats and calves, but by his own blood he entered in once into the holy place, having obtained eternal redemption for us. For if the blood of bulls and of goats, and the ashes of an heifer sprinkling the unclean, sanctifieth to the purifying of the flesh: how much more shall THE BLOOD OF CHRIST, who through the eternal Spirit offered himself without spot to God, purge your conscience from dead works to serve the living God? Hebrews 9:12-14

Jesus, our High Priest, has a ministry with His blood. This is an awesome truth. Because of the blood of Jesus, we have access to God.

After Jesus' blood was shed, He personally carried it into the heavenly Holy of Holies, where it was placed on the Mercy Seat of Heaven for our sins. That blood has never lost its power to redeem.

The natural blood that flows in our bodies does many things for us, and many of those same things are done for us in a spiritual sense by the blood of Jesus. For instance, our natural blood cleanses our bodies, removing toxins and other forms of waste. Nothing cleanses like the blood of Jesus. It washes *"white as snow."*

Our natural blood nourishes the physical body. When we eat, the nourishment from the digested food is passed into the bloodstream, and the blood carries it to every part of the body. When we breathe, the oxygen in the air is taken into the blood, and the blood then carries that oxygen to every cell in our bodies. Nothing nourishes us, and thus refreshes and renews us, like the blood of Jesus.

Our natural blood provides a protection for our physical bodies. When germs enter the body from any source, certain blood cells instantly begin to fight them. The blood of Jesus does this same thing for us.

Many of the vaccinations we receive against certain illnesses are actually a mild form of the disease. When that vaccine is injected into our systems, the blood goes to work instantly building up antibodies, forming an immunity to the disease.

When they first began developing a smallpox vaccine, the process was still rather primitive. They would actually take the vaccine from infected people. It had to be taken at just the right stage of the illness, and the vaccines gathered in this way could not be stored long or they spoiled.

When there was a sudden outbreak of smallpox in South America, European doctors began to search for ways to get the smallpox vaccine from Europe to South America in time to save lives. Travel was done in those days by ship, however, and crossing the ocean took many days. The solution they arrived at was quite innovative and touching.

They took twelve young boys from a poor house (the youngest of them was just three), injected two of them with the smallpox virus and then put them all on a ship bound for South America. When the two boys' sickness had reached just the right stage, they gathered enough smallpox vaccine from them to inoculate two more. With these two, they inoculated two more and continued doing this. In this way, they reached South America with living smallpox virus and were able to save thousands of lives there. Later, a monument was built to honor those twelve boys who had sacrificed to make it all happen. Immunization is a powerful tool.

The first time I went to Africa, I had to be immunized against yellow fever. Before the clinic personnel would give me the shot, they made me sign a form saying that I released them from all responsibility for possible side effects. The seventh possible side effect on the list was "death." Signing my name to that form could have been a scary thing, but I told the nurse, "I'm taking this in Jesus' name." And it worked. I could actually feel it when the vaccine took effect.

The blood of Jesus changes things. When it was carried into the heavenly Holy of Holies, Satan trembled. He was defeated. He could not resist the blood of Jesus:

> *And they overcame him by the blood of the Lamb, and by the word of their testimony; and they loved not their lives unto the death.*
>
> Revelation 12:11

When we hear these truths, understand them, believe them in our hearts, let them renew our minds and put them into our mouths, we are armed for battle. We can overcome Satan because he cannot pass the blood line.

Many phrases have been developed concerning the blood, and one of the most common is to "plead" the blood. This word *plead* is also a courtroom term. When you are in a legal situation in a courtroom before a judge, you want a good lawyer to plead your case so that you can be found innocent. Jesus' blood works for our defense.

To plead the blood means to make the blood effective, or to enforce the blood covenant. It means to put into legal standing the promises of God concerning His blood. Jesus, through the sacrifice of His blood, has defeated Satan. Therefore, we plead the blood of Jesus against our enemies. It is His blood that cleanses us from all sin — not only the sin of the past, but also its domination in the present and future.

Hebrews has much to say about the blood. It speaks of the Lord purging our consciences *"from dead works"* in order *"to serve the living God."* In my Bible, I have this word *"from"* underlined. The blood of Jesus cleanses us *"from"* dead works and gives us the forgiveness of sins, and thank God for that — but there is more.

If I were just delivered, if I were just forgiven of my sins and left there, I would still not be motivated to serve God. The blood works in us to motivate us *"to serve the living God."* We are taken *"from"* something and directed *"to"* something. This is a good *"from,"* and it is also a good *"to."*

The power of the blood is not only for a onetime salvation experience. It continues to be effective throughout our Christian lives:

> *If we confess our sins, he is faithful and just to forgive us our sins and to cleanse us from all unrighteousness.*　　1 John 1:9

We receive not only forgiveness, but cleansing from

past sins. And then God removes the record of it from His mind. Suddenly, it no longer exists.

This is a miracle, for God is all-knowing. He willingly lays aside His power in this regard when it comes to our sins. He chooses not to know, not to remember. Our sins are removed so far from Him that He cannot remember them any longer. Thank God for that great miracle!

Many other scriptures confirm these truths. For instance:

> *And you hath he quickened, who were dead in trespasses and sins; wherein in time past ye walked according to the course of this world, according to the prince of the power of the air, the spirit that now worketh in the children of disobedience: among whom also we all had our conversation in times past in the lusts of our flesh, fulfilling the desires of the flesh and of the mind; and were by nature the children of wrath, even as others.*
>
> Ephesians 2:1-3

> *In whom we have redemption through his blood, even the forgiveness of sins.*   Colossians 1:14

If you are still struggling with your past life, you do not have a revelation of the blood of Jesus and its cleansing effect. When a person dies, we bury him.

We would not want to leave a dead person lying around the house or in the public places we frequent, and we certainly would not want to be digging a dead person up again. What a terrible job that would be! Just think of the rot, the decay and the stench! Yuk!

Still, this is exactly what we do when we constantly bring up our past lives. We're digging up the putrid past, the rottenness of our former lives. If we have been cleansed by the blood of Jesus, it's time to leave that which is dead buried. It is no longer necessary for us to struggle with the past. Jesus paid the price for our sins. Why should we pay that price again ... and again and again?

Jesus has defeated Satan. Why should we struggle with him every day? None of us is smart enough or strong enough to struggle with the devil, and we don't have to. Get a revelation of what Christ has done for you and what He is doing for you RIGHT NOW, and you can be free of these struggles. You are *"a new creature"*:

> *Therefore if any man be in Christ, he is a new creature: old things are passed away; behold, all things are become new.* 2 Corinthians 5:17

Get a revelation of this truth. If God says He will not remember your sins anymore, why should you remember them? If they are under the blood, why dredge them back up again? We are no longer weak and helpless. The precious blood of Jesus cleanses us *"from dead works"* and it also empowers us *"to serve the living God."* He not only cleanses me *"from"* something, but His blood motivates me *"to"* something.

Few passages in the Bible have changed my life like Hebrews 13:20-21 has:

> *Now the God of peace, that brought again from the dead our Lord Jesus, that great shepherd of the sheep, through the blood of the everlasting covenant, make you perfect in every good work to do his will, working in you that which is well-pleasing in his sight, through Jesus Christ; to whom be glory for ever and ever. Amen.*
>
> Hebrews 13:20-21

Paul also wrote to the Philippians:

> *For it is God which worketh in you both to will and to do of his good pleasure.*
>
> Philippians 2:13

As believers, we have many tools at our disposal. We have the power of the Holy Spirit, we have the authority of the name of Jesus, we have the Word of God, and we have the blood of Jesus. When you consider all that God has given us and how they all work together, there is no way that we should fail.

It was a revelation on the blood of Jesus that brought me into the ministry. After I had been filled with the Spirit, the Lord sent me to a church that had a woman preacher. I had never seen that before, and I didn't believe in women being preachers.

I was particularly offended by *this* particular woman. I didn't like the way she looked; I didn't like the way she dressed; I didn't like the way she sounded. She had preached so often without the use of a microphone that she had developed a very deep voice that grated on me. She would walk back and forth across the platform waving a white handkerchief and preaching and praising God in that deep voice. Oh, how very strange that was for me!

I had recently read in a book that I should just tell God what I was thinking because He knows it anyway. So, that's the way I prayed in those days. I have learned better since then. Now I know that I should pray what God thinks, not what I think. His thoughts are so much higher than mine that He doesn't need to hear what I think; I need to hear what He thinks. Later, I also learned to pray His Word, but at this point in my life, I hadn't yet heard of that concept.

During the time I had sought the Holy Spirit baptism, someone said that the devil would take the things dearest to your heart and use them against you. I committed all the things dearest to my heart (my husband and my children) to God, and I did receive the Holy Spirit. I wondered if that meant I might lose them at some point, at least that's the fear Satan put into my heart.

I went to the lady pastor for counseling, and she said to me, "You're going to be a preacher too. I used to be just as bashful and timid as you are, but look what God has done for me. He's going to do the same thing for you." When she said that, a terrible rebellion rose up within me. *Dear God, no!* I thought, *Surely You wouldn't do that to me.*

The devil said to me, "Now God is going to kill your husband, and you'll have to go to a part of Africa that has many snakes." Not only did I not want to go to Africa; I didn't want to be a preacher at all, and I told God so.

"I'm not going," I insisted. "And I'm not going to be a preacher either."

But as I read Hebrews 13:20-21 in my daily devotions, it began to change my thinking entirely. (In fact, this powerful passage is still changing my life.) I learned to pray from that passage. As I prayed, I still told God that I didn't want to be a preacher, but I did it in a little different way. "Lord, I don't want to be a woman preacher," I told Him, "but I see here in Your Word that You're able to work through the blood in me and make me perfect in every good work to do

Your will, working in me all that's well-pleasing. I commit my will to You. Work by the blood in my will and my 'want to.' "

And He did. Before long, my "want to" had been dramatically changed. Today, the greatest satisfaction I receive is from preaching God's Word. It is never a chore. I love to do it; I want to do it more and more; I would die if I couldn't preach the Word of God. I'd rather preach God's Word than play with my grandchildren – and that is saying a lot.

This is how powerful the blood of Jesus is! What I once dreaded is now a very holy thing to me. It is clearly my greatest desire in life, as unnatural as that sounds. This is a work of grace the Lord has done in me by the blood of Jesus.

If you're struggling with your willpower, you haven't understood the Gospel. If you're struggling in this way, you need to hear the good news that Jesus is living for us as our High Priest. The blood He shed for us was not just for the forgiveness of our sins. It was to enable us to perform good works, to do the will of God.

Through Christ's blood, He purges our "want to." He works in us until His desires become our desires. What a supernatural experience! *"It is God that works in us both to will and to do of His good pleasure."* We don't have to struggle anymore with the devil. He's defeated. We don't even have to struggle with our will because of the precious blood of Jesus.

I give glory to God for this good, new covenant. It is failure-proof. It is perfect. Jesus is the resurrected Lord of Glory, and He is our High Priest, our Savior. He became the sin offering for us, but now He is living to make effective that which He purchased when He died for us and when He shed His precious blood.

Chapter Sixteen

He Is Living as Guarantor of the New Covenant

For men verily swear by the greater: and an oath for confirmation is to them an end of all strife. Wherein God, willing more abundantly to show unto the heirs of promise the immutability of his counsel, confirmed it by an oath.

Hebrews 6:16-17

By so much was Jesus MADE A SURETY of a better testament.   Hebrews 7:22

Jesus, our High Priest, is living as the Guarantor of the New Covenant. That's what makes this covenant failure-proof and perfect. As long as Jesus is alive, this covenant is guaranteed.

I have not been able to find another phrase in the Bible equal to *"willing more abundantly."* How much more could He want to do these things for us? When we speak of the will of God, we could mean some particular decree, or we might simply be referring to His desires. When God decrees something, nothing you can do will change it. His strongest desire for us (*"willing more abundantly"*) is to *"show the heirs of the promise the immutability [the unchangeableness, the absoluteness] of his counsel."*

The writer continued:

> *That by two immutable things, in which it was impossible for God to lie, we might have a strong consolation, who have fled for refuge to lay hold upon the hope set before us: which hope we have as an anchor of the soul, both sure and stedfast, and which entereth into that within the veil.*
>
> Hebrews 6:18-19

We need to have a strong, settled assurance of the unchangeableness of the absoluteness of God's Word, and our Guarantor is Jesus Himself. God made an oath to Abraham:

> *By myself have I sworn, saith the LORD, for because thou hast done this thing, and hast not withheld thy son, thine only son: that in blessing I will bless thee, and in multiplying I will multiply thy seed as the stars of the heaven, and as the sand*

which is upon the sea shore; and thy seed shall possess the gate of his enemies; and in thy seed shall all the nations of the earth be blessed; because thou hast obeyed my voice.

Genesis 22:16-18

This word *"sworn"* means "to swear, as if repeating a declaration seven times over." Jesus is the living Guarantor of God's Word and its unchangeableness. It is absolutely true. He swore an oath to Abraham.

We know that when God proclaims something, even one time, it comes into existence; it suddenly is. He said, *"Let there be light,"* and light is still in existence after many thousands of years. Light is still expanding, although we can barely comprehend the truth of that fact. God didn't have to say, "I'm going to say it again: 'Let there be light!' " No, He only had to say it one time. And when He said it, there was light, and there still is light.

As long as Jesus is alive, we have His guarantee. What a blessing! His Word is sure and it never fails.

Jesus came to earth and possessed the gate of our enemies so that He could set us free. Because He lives, we live also. Before this promise of God could die, Jesus would have to die, and that simply isn't going to happen. He is living to make good the promise given to Abraham, that in blessing He would bless you and in multiplying He would multiply you. He has delivered you from the hand of all your enemies. He is swearing seven times over so that you can have strong assurance. He is the Guarantor.

Because Hell could not hold Jesus, the gates of Hell now cannot prevail against us. Have a strong assurance. He is the Guarantor. He is the surety of this better covenant. As long as Jesus is alive, He is making good His covenant with us.

Chapter Seventeen

He Is Living to Perfect Our Faith

Looking unto Jesus the author and FINISHER OF OUR FAITH; who for the joy that was set before him endured the cross, despising the shame, and is set down at the right hand of the throne of God. Hebrews 12:2

Jesus, our High Priest, is living to perfect our faith. Just as He is the *"author"* of faith, He is also the *"finisher"* of it.

I can look back over my own life and see when faith first came to me. Then, through the years, as I heard the Word of God, more faith came to me. This has always been accompanied by manifestations of great joy. Still today, my faith is growing, and now I am able to receive more than I could when I first came to Jesus.

This does not mean that God loves me any more now than before. He loves us all with an intense love, and He loves us all the time. But I am now able to receive more than I could before.

There are many levels of faith. For instance, it is said of Moses that he knew God's *"ways,"* whereas the other children of Israel only knew *"His acts"*:

> *He made known his ways unto Moses, his acts unto the children of Israel.* Psalm 103:7

The children of Israel knew God on this one level, but Moses knew God on a completely different level. I have known people who experienced great things in God, great miracles or great manifestations, but they still did not seem to really know God intimately. They were inspired by God's *"acts,"* but for some reason, they seemed to have no interest in His *"ways."* For instance, many people receive miraculous physical healings, and yet they never truly give their hearts to the Lord to serve Him. There are many levels of faith, and the Lord is willing to *"finish,"* or perfect, our faith if we desire it.

Jesus is living to perfect your faith, and He knows just what you need. You might think your faith is very small, but if you have Jesus living to perfect it and put the finishing touches on it, you can go much farther in faith.

Without faith we cannot please God:

He Is Living to Perfect Our Faith

But without faith it is impossible to please him: for he that cometh to God must believe that he is, and that he is a rewarder of them that diligently seek him. Hebrews 11:6

And the more faith we have, the closer we can get to Him. Therefore, let Him work in you to grow your faith and perfect it. He is living for that purpose.

Chapter Eighteen

He Is Living to Preside Over Our Gifts and Sacrifices

By him therefore let us offer THE SACRIFICE OF PRAISE to God continually, that is, the fruit of our lips giving thanks to his name. But to do good and to communicate forget not: for with such sacrifices God is well pleased.

Hebrews 13:15-16

Jesus, our High Priest, is living to preside over our gifts and sacrifices. This is an important truth.

The sacrifices we offer to God today are very different from those of the Old Testament. Many of them were related to blood, for forgiveness, and the sacrifice of Christ once and for all has made that type of sacrifice unnecessary.

Our most important sacrifice to God is *"the fruit of our lips."* We are not to praise Him just when we feel like it; we are to do it *"continually."* He has called us to *"give thanks to His name."*

Beyond this, there is more to our sacrifice to God. We are told *"to do good and to communicate forget not."* We know what *"to do good"* means, and we need to do more of it. Jesus *"went about doing good"* (Acts 10:38), and we are called to do the same.

This word *"communicate"* not only refers to fellowship, but it also refers to our material giving, our tithes and our offerings. Such giving is part of our service to God, part of our worship to Him.

Many Christians have learned to tithe, but they still have not realized their giving is part of their worship. If we could all understand that Jesus has a ministry with our tithes and offerings, and that these things are holy, a sweet smelling offering that expresses our love to Him, it would transform our lives and make our giving much more meaningful.

As we learn this, let us become better givers and, thus, better worshippers. Our High Priest is awaiting our sacrifices today.

Part IV:

God's Hidden Agenda

Chapter Nineteen

Lucifer's Fall

Son of man, take up a lamentation upon the king of Tyrus, and say unto him, Thus saith the Lord GOD; Thou sealest up the sum, full of wisdom, and perfect in beauty. Ezekiel 28:12

Ezekiel recorded the origin of Satan (formerly Lucifer), and among the many important things the prophet tells us about the enemy before his fall are these: he was *"full of wisdom,"* and he was *"perfect in beauty."* If Satan was *"full of wisdom,"* as a created being, that wisdom had to be from God, but something happened to that wisdom, and it became corrupted. What could it have been?

The passage goes on to show us the lavishness God had invested in Lucifer:

Thou hast been in Eden the garden of God; every precious stone was thy covering, the sardius, to-

> *paz, and the diamond, the beryl, the onyx, and*
> *the jasper, the sapphire, the emerald, and the car-*
> *buncle, and gold: the workmanship of thy tabrets*
> *and of thy pipes was prepared in thee in the day*
> *that thou wast created.*   Ezekiel 28:13

Precious jewels had covered Lucifer since the day he was created, and he was designed with musical instruments as part of his being. He was a glorious creation.

Lucifer was honored in Heaven as *"the anointed cherub that covereth"* and much more:

> *Thou art the anointed cherub that covereth; and I*
> *have set thee so: thou wast upon the holy moun-*
> *tain of God; thou hast walked up and down in*
> *the midst of the stones of fire. Thou wast perfect*
> *in thy ways from the day that thou wast created,*
> *till iniquity was found in thee.*
>   Ezekiel 28:14-15

This is the point in the narrative when things began to go wrong. Until this point, Lucifer had been *"per-fect."* He was the leader of Heaven's choirs, and God had given him a very high place in the scheme of things. Now, however, *"iniquity was found in [Lucifer],"* and in the very next verse, God was casting him out of His holy mountain. What was this *"iniquity"* that caused Lucifer's fall?

> *Thine heart was lifted up because of thy beauty,*
> *thou hast corrupted thy wisdom ... .*
> Ezekiel 28:17

Lucifer's heart was *"lifted up,"* meaning that he became proud, and this pride resulted in the corruption of his wisdom. Pride is nothing more than corrupted wisdom, and corrupted wisdom is nothing more than pride.

Isaiah also had something to say about the origin of Satan:

> *How art thou fallen from heaven, O Lucifer, son*
> *of the morning! how art thou cut down to the*
> *ground, which didst weaken the nations! For thou*
> *hast said in thine heart, I will ascend into heaven,*
> *I will exalt my throne above the stars of God: I*
> *will sit also upon the mount of the congregation,*
> *in the sides of the north: I will ascend above the*
> *heights of the clouds; I will be like the most High.*
> *Yet thou shalt be brought down to hell, to the sides*
> *of the pit.* Isaiah 14:12-15

It is very clear that Lucifer fell from his exalted place and became Satan because of pride. Pride led him to think that he could rise higher than God Himself. This mistaken notion brought him *"down to Hell."* He was created to give praise to God, but he decided that he wanted to exalt himself instead.

Pride is anything that tries to exalt itself against God. It is anything that tries to replace God's throne with Satan's. And many of the other enemies we struggle with on a daily basis are related to pride.

For instance, what is fear? When we are afraid of something, it means that we are exalting Satan's lies above God's truth. Fear is actually another form of pride. If we know God's greatness, how can we be afraid?

What is worry? It is a low-grade fear, and if you continually yield to it, it will develop into full-blown fear in your life. It is nothing more than pride. When you succumb to worry, you are exalting Satan's lies above God's truth.

What about murmuring? It can also be placed under the category of pride. Murmuring results when we exalt Satan's throne above God.

There are many other ways that we can express pride. Too many people, for example, stand up in church and say, "Please pray for me. The devil has been after me all week. Pray that I will hold out until the end." When they do that, they are actually giving glory to the devil. If you are afraid of the devil or of what he can do, you are playing right into his hands.

You are exalting him, and he loves it. If you're thinking of the devil as bigger than God, or exalting your problems or your sicknesses and considering them bigger than God, you're exalting Satan above God and getting into pride. It's that simple.

We're not talking about sinners now. Many people who love God unknowingly exalt Satan above Him. They have their focus on how strong the devil is. To talk to them, you would think that the devil is the strongest, most powerful being in existence. Without even realizing it, they are giving him glory, and they are exalting him above God. This, of course, is dangerous, and nothing good can come of it. Let God put wisdom in your heart today in this regard.

Lucifer was the first transgressor, not Adam. He wanted to be like God. He wanted to exalt his throne *"above the stars of God."* Pride caused his downfall.

The name *Lucifer* means "the bright and shining one," and he was indeed a rising star in God's presence. After his fall, however, he became *Satan,* which means "adversary." By trying to rise higher than God, Lucifer (now Satan) became the enemy of God and the enemy of God's people.

Now, Satan has no more light. He masquerades as *"an angel of light"* (2 Corinthians 11:14), but he is anything but an angel and anything but light.

When he came to Eve in Eden, he decided to play

upon the same weakness that caused his own downfall. The first temptation he used was a call to her pride.

Next, Satan cast doubt on the Word of God and contradicted what God had said. He told Eve that if she would do what he was suggesting, rather than what God had said, she would become like God. This was the same twisted wisdom that had brought him *"down to Hell,"* and he now hoped to drag mankind down with him.

When Eve looked at the tree and saw that it looked harmless, and when she heard that eating the fruit of it would make her wise, she was hooked. Satan had thus become a gifted deceiver and a polished liar and he has been honing those skills ever since. He is great at offering what he cannot deliver and proposing what he cannot fulfill.

Satan's judgment was immediate. He was cast out from the presence of the Lord. He was judged and cursed in the Garden of Eden. He was further judged on the cross. In Christ's death and resurrection, He defeated Satan and took his authority away from him. The King James Bible says that Jesus *"destroy[ed] him that had the power of death"*:

> *Forasmuch then as the children are partakers of flesh and blood, he also himself likewise took part of the same; that through death he might destroy him that had the power of death, that is, the devil.*
>
> Hebrews 2:14

Most modern Bible versions translate this word *"destroy"* as *"render powerless."* The Emphasized New Testament: A New Translation by Joseph Bryant Rotherham (© 1959 by Kregel Publications, Grand Rapids, Michigan) goes even further. It declares that the Lord fully intended *"to paralyze him [Satan]."*

Now Satan has become nothing more than *"the god of this world"*:

> *The god of this world has blinded the minds of the unbelieving, that they might not see the light of the gospel of the glory of Christ, who is the image of God.* 2 Corinthians 4:4, NAS

So, *"the god of this world"* is nothing more than a lying, thieving, bumbling failure who delights in seeing others fail as he has. He has no real power, so the only way he can achieve this is by deceiving men into thinking that they are gods themselves. He was already cursed when he approached Eve in the garden, but he continues to draw prideful men and women to his side, fallen creature that he is.

Chapter Twenty

A Devil Shield

But he giveth more grace. Wherefore he saith, God resisteth the proud, but giveth grace unto the humble. Submit yourselves therefore to God. Resist the devil, and he will flee from you. James 4:6-7

Even though Satan is disarmed, he still exists, and he is still a danger to every believer. I see two common errors among Christians in this regard. Far too many believers fear Satan, and he is not to be feared. He is already defeated, and we must rejoice in that defeat. Then, there are those who ignore Satan entirely – as if he didn't exist at all. If we ignore Satan, he will eat (*"devour"*) us. Both of these extremes are in error. What we must do is develop a shield against him.

We already know that we are on the winning side:

And I say also unto thee, That thou art Peter, and

upon this rock I will build my church; and the gates of hell shall not prevail against it.
                                    Matthew 16:18

And the God of peace shall bruise Satan under your feet shortly.   Romans 16:20

For he must reign, till he hath put all enemies under his feet.   1 Corinthians 15:25

So, what is our most effective shield against Satan? God spoke to me one day and said, "Humility is a devil shield." It happened in the following way:

I have a television program in our town, but some months ago we began to have problems with our camera. We sent it away for repair, and it came back with a note saying that (although they charged us for the service) they hadn't found anything wrong with the camera. It turned out that the camera was encountering interference from the many antennas installed on our mountain.

Because I live high up on a mountain, there are television antennas, radio antennas, pager antennas and cell phone antennas all around us. One evening, I counted fourteen of them near our house. The pagers, especially, were a problem for our television equipment.

After we found out what the problem was, a precious Spirit-filled brother who was helping us offered to build a shield around the camera to protect it from all the interference. But try as he might, he couldn't find anything that would protect us from the many signals bouncing around that mountaintop.

Finally, I got fed up with the problem one day. In my soft Mississippi voice, I took authority over the devil and over all that interference. I especially spoke against the pagers that were causing us so much trouble.

The next day, the headline in the *Meridian Star* was: SATELLITE OUTAGE STOPS PAGER SERVICE NATIONWIDE. The article went on to say, "Millions of pagers that keep doctors, detectives and loved ones in touch stopped working nationwide when a $250 million communication satellite suddenly lost track of the earth. The Galaxy Four satellite stopped relaying pager messages as well as behind-the-scenes television communications at about 6 p.m. Tuesday, when its onboard control system and a backup switch failed, and the satellite rotated out of its proper position. Technicians were able to send commands to the craft, but failed to restore its proper orientation to earth."

They were having a hard time figuring out what went wrong, but I knew. Someone had taken authority over the interference in Jesus' name. That was very exciting. It was while I was reading that article that the Holy Ghost said to me: "Humility is a devil shield."

What does that mean? It means that Satan doesn't know how to penetrate humility, because it is so contrary to everything that he is. So, if we can arm ourselves with true humility, we can better protect ourselves against all the wiles of the devil.

Most Christians don't yet understand what true humility is. It is not weakness, and it is not a sense of somehow being inferior. You don't have to develop an inferiority complex to be humble. The greatest of all beings is the humblest of all. Jesus is the example of true humility.

This is something we want to understand. After that, I noticed that every time God speaks in His Word of resisting the devil, He also speaks of humility. The two go together.

Before the writer of Hebrews said, *"Resist the devil, and he will flee from you,"* he first said, *"God resisteth the proud, but giveth grace unto the humble."* And his conclusion was: *"Submit yourselves therefore to God"* or "Humble yourselves before God."

In our theme verse for this chapter, James wrote: *"He [God] giveth more grace."* And to whom does He give it? The Amplified Bible renders the response as: *"those who are humble enough to receive it."*

Peter also witnessed to this truth of the direct connection between humility and defeating the devil. First, he spoke of the need for humility:

Likewise, ye younger, submit yourselves unto the elder. Yea, all of you be subject one to another, and be clothed with humility: for God resisteth the proud, and giveth grace to the humble. Humble yourselves therefore under the mighty hand of God, that he may exalt you in due time.

1 Peter 5:5-6

Next, he told us how to humble ourselves:

Casting all your care upon him; for he careth for you. 1 Peter 5:7

Finally, Peter warned:

Be sober, be vigilant; because your adversary the devil, as a roaring lion, walketh about, seeking whom he may devour: whom resist stedfast in the faith, knowing that the same afflictions are accomplished in your brethren that are in the world. But the God of all grace, who hath called us unto his eternal glory by Christ Jesus, after that ye have suffered a while, make you perfect, stablish, strengthen, settle you. 1 Peter 5:8-10

The proverbs are rich in teaching about the destructive power of pride:

When pride cometh, then cometh shame: but with the lowly is wisdom. Proverbs 11:2

Only by pride cometh contention: but with the well advised is wisdom. Proverbs 13:10

In the mouth of the foolish is a rod of pride: but the lips of the wise shall preserve them.
Proverbs 14:3

Pride goeth before destruction, and an haughty spirit before a fall. Better it is to be of an humble spirit with the lowly, than to divide the spoil with the proud. Proverbs 16:18-19

He that is of a proud heart stirreth up strife: but he that putteth his trust in the LORD shall be made fat. Proverbs 28:25

A man's pride shall bring him low: but honour shall uphold the humble in spirit.
Proverbs 29:23

When we allow pride to enter into our lives and we exalt self, there will surely be a fall. Pride invariably brings on a fall. This fact was revealed most strikingly in the life of King Nebuchadnezzar of Babylon. When he decided that his own genius and ability had gotten him the kingdom, he received word (through the interpretation of a dream brought to him by Daniel) that he was about to lose everything.

And Nebuchadnezzar did lose everything – even his sanity. The Scriptures say of him:

> *All this came upon the king Nebuchadnezzar.*
> Daniel 4:28

Within a year after Daniel had spoken, Nebuchadnezzar was wandering the fields like some wild animal, and he stayed that way until he recognized that God ruled and set whomever He would over the nations. When he humbled himself, he was restored. He later wrote:

> *And at the end of the days I Nebuchadnezzar lifted up mine eyes unto heaven, and mine understanding returned unto me, and I blessed the most High, and I praised and honoured him that liveth for ever, whose dominion is an everlasting dominion, and his kingdom is from generation to generation: and all the inhabitants of the earth are reputed as nothing: and he doeth according to his will in the army of heaven, and among the inhabitants of the earth: and none can stay his hand, or say unto him, What doest thou?*
> *At the same time my reason returned unto me;*

and for the glory of my kingdom, mine honour and brightness returned unto me; and my counsellors and my lords sought unto me; and I was established in my kingdom, and excellent majesty was added unto me. Now I Nebuchadnezzar praise and extol and honour the King of heaven, all whose works are truth, and his ways judgment: and those that walk in pride he is able to abase.

Daniel 4:34-37

The sad thing is that Nebuchadnezzar had to learn humility the hard way. Jesus is our example. He chose to humble Himself:

Let this mind be in you, which was also in Christ Jesus: who, being in the form of God, thought it not robbery to be equal with God: but made himself of no reputation, and took upon him the form of a servant, and was made in the likeness of men: and being found in fashion as a man, he humbled himself, and became obedient unto death, even the death of the cross.   Philippians 2:5-8

That God would choose to do this for you and me is an awesome truth that should humble every one of us.

What happened to Jesus as a result of His humility should be a lesson to us all as well:

> *Wherefore God also hath highly exalted him, and given him a name which is above every name: that at the name of Jesus every knee should bow, of things in heaven, and things in earth, and things under the earth; and that every tongue should confess that Jesus Christ is Lord, to the glory of God the Father.* Philippians 2:9-11

Humility = promotion. Humility is never inferiority. If you have any feelings of unworthiness, you can know where they came from: the pit of Hell. True humility leads us to certain exaltation.

Most of us have not yet understood what true humility is, but we must learn. Although we try to use many other methods against the enemy, humility is always our greatest defense against him.

Many years ago, when I first started in ministry, some people were saying some things about me that were not true. That angered me so that when I began praying about it I actually spit at the devil. I felt so strange at that moment that I prayed, "Lord, what do You think about that?"

He didn't answer me at all at that moment. Later that day, He did answer. "When you did that," He said, "it did not affect the devil at all. In fact, you were getting over into his way of accomplishing things. It is My Word in your mouth that will defeat the devil. He can't flee far enough into the depths of Hell to get away from it. Humble your heart, and I will give you victory over the devil."

That word was as strong as anything I have ever heard from the Lord, and I have never been able to forget it. At first, what the Lord said about humbling my heart didn't seem to make sense to me. Other people were hurting me, and I was the one who needed to humble my heart? I realized in that moment that I didn't really understand what true humility was, and I began to search the Word of God for understanding.

Although I have now been studying the Bible for more than thirty years, it was only recently that I began to see this truth clearly. I would read what the Bible said about resisting the devil, and I would read what the Bible said about humility for the believer, but I had never connected the two things before. Now, I am realizing more every day how very important it is to our victory over the evil one.

After I began to learn about true humility, I found that one of the fruits of humility is honoring others. My humility must not only be before God, but also before men. When I began to honor others as the Word of God teaches, I was amazed at the result. Many tense situations were relieved, and I began to grow more rapidly in my spiritual life.

Humility is a devil shield. He doesn't know what to

do with it. It is so opposed to his nature that it repels him. Because he works through our pride, humility is an effective shield against him.

God's Word presents us with many paradoxes: We must die to live. We must give to get. We must humble ourselves to be promoted. We must go down in order to go up. When someone wrongs us, we must turn the other cheek to him or her. We must forgive in order to be forgiven. The devil cannot break through this shield of humility.

If we choose to humble ourselves, then God won't have to humble us:

> *And whosoever shall exalt himself shall be abased;*
> *and he that shall humble himself shall be exalted.*
> Matthew 23:12

If we choose to judge ourselves, then we won't have to be judged:

> *For if we would judge ourselves, we should not be*
> *judged.* 1 Corinthians 11:31

Make the decision to be *"clothed with humility,"* and you'll never be sorry.

Pride causes men not to seek God:

> *The wicked, through the pride of his countenance,*

will not seek after God: God is not in all his
thoughts.   Psalm 10:4

But even God's people have a problem in this regard. God tells us to call on Him:

If my people, which are called by my name, shall
humble themselves, and pray, and seek my face,
and turn from their wicked ways; then will I hear
from heaven, and will forgive their sin, and will
heal their land.   2 Chronicles 7:14

The very act of calling on God is prayer is an act of humility. When we call upon Him, we are saying, "Lord, we can't do it without You." And when we take that attitude, we suddenly find that we *"can do all things through [Him]"* (Philippians 4:13).

Refusing to praise God is also an act of pride. Prideful people don't like praise, and the devil is determined to stop it. Pastors tell me that they have more problems with worship leaders, musicians and singers than with anything else in their churches. Satan hates worship and will do anything he can to stop it.

When Jesus made His triumphal entry into Jerusalem and the people laid palm branches in His pathway and sang praises to His name, many of the religious leaders of the day didn't like it. They tried to silence the crowd.

If we want God to dwell among us, we must become those who know true humility:

> *For thus saith the high and lofty One that inhabiteth eternity, whose name is Holy; I dwell in the high and holy place, with him also that is of a contrite and humble spirit, to revive the spirit of the humble, and to revive the heart of the contrite ones.*　　　　Isaiah 57:15

You won't find a better devil shield.

Chapter Twenty-One

The Hidden Agenda for the Church

To the intent that now unto the principalities and powers in heavenly places might be known BY THE CHURCH the manifold wisdom of God.
Ephesians 3:10

God's plan is to use His Church to show forth His wisdom. This is certainly humiliating for the devil, and we want to see why. It is part of his progressive judgment.

Satan was judged in the Garden of Eden, he was judged at Calvary, and he will suffer a final judgment. The Lake of Fire was especially prepared for him and those who ally themselves with him. I applaud God's wisdom in this, for Satan surely deserves the Lake of Fire. But I applaud God even more for His great plan that reveals the glory of His wisdom day by day through humble men and women everywhere. Every day Satan is being judged as he is forced to witness

God revealing His true wisdom through common men and women. This is God's hidden agenda.

I have noticed this hidden agenda being mentioned again and again throughout the New Testament. God has empowered His little ones, the humblest of men and women, to show Satan and every principality and power His wisdom. This work will not be done by heavenly creatures but *"by the Church."* That includes you and me.

Before He left the earth, Jesus offered His power and authority to common men and women. He said:

> *All power is given unto me in heaven and in earth.*
> *Go ye therefore, and teach all nations, baptizing*
> *them in the name of the Father, and of the Son,*
> *and of the Holy Ghost.*   Matthew 28:18-19

The first thing Jesus told His disciples to do after they had received the power of the Holy Spirit was to *"cast out devils"*:

> *And these signs shall follow them that believe; In*
> *my name shall they cast out devils ... .*
> Mark 16:17

Isn't that wonderful? God has given us, His little ones, power and authority over Satan and all his demons as part of their ongoing judgment and punishment.

The men God chose to use in Bible days were not superhuman, as some suppose. Paul, for instance, spoke often of his limitations:

> *Whereof I was made a minister, according to the gift of the grace of God given unto me by the effectual working of his power. Unto me, who am less than the least of all saints, is this grace given, that I should preach among the Gentiles the unsearchable riches of Christ.*
>
> Ephesians 3:7-8

Paul was not suffering from an inferiority complex. He was just stating the facts. Unlike those who would promote humanism and total self-confidence, telling us that we are all gods and all we have to do is look inside ourselves for the answer to every problem, Paul knew that he needed the Lord.

It was only a few verses later that Paul identified God's hidden agenda, that *"the manifold wisdom of God"* might be made known *"now unto the principalities and powers,"* and that it might be done *"by the Church."* God wants to demonstrate His power and wisdom through insignificant people, so that Lucifer and all spiritual principalities and powers will tremble and be ashamed. God's way is to use the weakest vessels to show forth His mighty strength.

Paul himself was not an eloquent person, and he did not have a powerful presentation. Other men said of him:

> *For his letters, say they, are weighty and power-ful; but his bodily presence is weak, and his speech contemptible.*   2 Corinthians 10:10

One of the most important things stressed by those who teach secular leadership is that we need to have a commanding presence. I made the mistake of attending several secular workshops and seminars on leadership, and came away disgusted with their humanistic approach to leadership. They tell us to assert ourselves, when God tells us just the opposite.

It blesses me to know that Paul was lacking in this regard, for he is one of my favorite Bible characters. If God could use him in the way He did, when *"his bodily presence [was] weak, and his speech contemptible,"* only God would receive the glory – and the devil received a black eye.

I am convinced that in the days to come we will see more Pauls being raised up, so that the wisdom of man can be confounded and Satan can be further brought to shame. God has chosen to show forth His great power through the very weakest of vessels. If you have ever thought, "Oh, I'm so weak. Surely I'm the weakest Christian around," you are a good candidate for

God's work. God will even use children in the days ahead, that He might be glorified.

Paul considered himself to be *"base"*:

> *Now I Paul myself beseech you by the meekness and gentleness of Christ, who in presence am base among you, but being absent am bold toward you.*
> 2 Corinthians 10:1

If we were placing qualifications on those who could work for the Lord, we would immediately think of those who were strong, well-educated and experienced. God sees it differently. What He is doing has nothing to do with our abilities. He delights in using those who lack ability, so that He receives the glory.

Paul wrote to the Corinthians:

> *For I am the least of the apostles, that am not meet to be called an apostle, because I persecuted the church of God. But by the grace of God I am what I am: and his grace which was bestowed upon me was not in vain; but I laboured more abundantly than they all: yet not I, but the grace of God which was with me.*
> 1 Corinthians 15:9-10

Part of this doesn't sound very humble, and some may think that Paul was boasting. But, clearly, he was boasting in the Lord, for he considered himself to be *"the least of the apostles"* and *"not meet [worthy] to be called an apostle."* If something was accomplished through Paul's ministry, it was by God's grace. If he *"laboured more abundantly than they all,"* it was because of *"the grace of God which was with [him]."*

So, God can use you too. If you are weak and insignificant or if you have failed over and over again, you're the perfect candidate to be used to free men and women from Satan's power. That's the Good News of the Gospel.

Paul wrote:

> *And he said unto me, My grace is sufficient for thee: for my strength is made perfect in weakness. Most gladly therefore will I rather glory in my infirmities, that the power of Christ may rest upon me. Therefore I take pleasure in infirmities, in reproaches, in necessities, in persecutions, in distresses for Christ's sake: for when I am weak, then am I strong.* 2 Corinthians 12:9-10

When God's *"strength"* is revealed *"in weakness,"* He gets all the glory. This is the reason He has instructed us to *"bestow more abundant honour"* upon those members among us that seem to be less significant:

> *And those members of the body, which we think to be less honourable, upon these we bestow more*

abundant honour; and our uncomely parts have more abundant comeliness. For our comely parts have no need: but God hath tempered the body together, having given more abundant honour to that part which lacked.

1 Corinthians 12:23-24

When I first read this passage of scripture, it didn't make sense to me. Why would God give the less honorable members more honor? But when I began to recognize His hidden agenda, it then made perfect sense. As part of Satan's judgment for allowing his wisdom to become corrupted through pride, God would use the Church to show forth His wisdom in the earth, and He would choose *"our uncomely parts"* to do this. God will use the Church to show the world how very good He is. He will show forth *"the exceeding riches of His grace"* and His kindness to us, and He has chosen the weakest among us to do it. God has chosen us as an object lesson to the age in which we live.

God's anointed cherub took his blessing for granted, lifted himself up in pride before God and had his wisdom corrupted as a result. He will regret it through eternity as he sees God using the most humble people of the earth to accomplish His eternal purposes.

For years, our state of Mississippi had a bad image around the country. People listened to our Southern accent and automatically looked down upon us as being poor and uneducated. One day I was speaking with a businessman in Meridian. He had just finished a telephone conversation with a man in California, and he was shaking his head. "They think we're nothing but a bunch of hicks," he said. "I told him I had to clean out my outhouse because black widow spiders were biting our behinds every time we used it – and he believed me!"

But God is changing our image. He is raising up His people throughout the length and breadth of the state and using them for His glory.

> *But God hath chosen the foolish things of the world to confound the wise; and God hath chosen the weak things of the world to confound the things which are mighty; and base things of the world, and things which are despised, hath God chosen, yea, and things which are not, to bring to nought things that are: that no flesh should glory in his presence.*   1 Corinthians 1:27-29

He has chosen *"the weak and foolish vessels to confound the wise."* That passage began in this way:

> *For ye see your calling, brethren, how that not many wise men after the flesh, not many mighty, not many noble, are called.*
>
> 1 Corinthians 1:26

Clearly God doesn't choose as we do. The great Welsh Revival of the early twentieth century came through Evan Roberts, a young man who quit school to begin preaching. His prayer base was made up of children, his co-workers were young people, and he was severely criticized by many of the church leaders of his day. When word got out of the great things God was doing, well-known men came from many directions, thinking that they could bring some direction to the burgeoning movement of the Holy Spirit. After they heard Evan Roberts preach, however, they remained seated and quiet in the presence of God. They were heard to say, "I could never have preached in the presence of God like we feel here." God was doing something wonderful, revealing Himself through the weakest of all.

Not long afterward, God poured out His Spirit at Azusa Street in Los Angeles, California. The man responsible for that outpouring that, like the Welsh Revival, affected the whole world (and continues to do so) was a humble black brother by the name of William Seymour. He was said to be ugly and so timid that he hid from others before and after services so that he would not have to socialize with them.

It was still a time of racial discrimination in America, and many churches would not have even allowed William Seymour to come into their churches. Yet, he was the vessel that God chose to use at Azusa Street.

People came to Los Angeles from all over the world and were blessed.

Today, our speakers are all spit and polish, but those of us who are hungry for more of God are ready to hear from someone who stutters now and then so that we can give God the glory for what is being done rather than only honor men and their gifts. God is choosing real, down-to-earth men.

It was said that Paul's speech was contemptible. Moses was a stutterer, as were Oral Roberts and Benny Hinn. Yet God chose them and used them.

Sometimes the devil tries to intimidate us: "Who do you think you are that God would use you?" But God says just the opposite. He is ready to show forth His glory through us.

I think we will be surprised in the future by whom God uses. One day soon, those who want to be healed may find themselves having small children lay hands on them. They would seem to be the most qualified in God's sight. What a wonderful day, when God is using those whom men would deem unqualified so that He can be glorified!

Some people are so proud of their ability to pray eloquently. But it's not a matter of being eloquent. Prayer is not something we have learned or memorized. It is an intimate communion with God, and even a child can do that. Your ability to speak beautiful words can never produce the miracles of God.

For years I meditated on Paul's words: *"For My*

strength is made perfect in weakness." The Amplified Bible says: *"My strength and power are made perfect (fulfilled and completed) and show themselves most effective in [your] weakness."*

The less qualified we feel, the more qualified we are to be used by God. Think of how that must frustrate Satan. It shakes him to the core when young people go out preaching and teaching and laying hands on the sick and seeing them recover, and when seemingly unqualified people cast out devils. God has a hidden agenda, to show forth His wisdom in this way.

In the high-tech world of today, prospective employees present their resumes to the personnel department of a company, and someone there looks them over carefully and then chooses the person he or she feels is best educated, with the most experience and the best presence. But that's not God's way. He chooses the weak and the foolish, because then He is glorified.

When Jesus was here on the earth, He chose simple men to do His work so that the Father could be glorified. He set the example by being born in a stable Himself. This gave us a clue to His hidden agenda for the future. Praise God that we are a part of it.

Chapter Twenty-Two

Satan's Sorrowful State and Our Glorious Future in Christ

Finally, my brethren, be strong in the Lord, and in the power of his might. Put on the whole armour of God, that ye may be able to stand against the wiles of the devil. For we wrestle not against flesh and blood, but against principalities, against powers, against the rulers of the darkness of this world, against spiritual wickedness in high places. Wherefore take unto you the whole armour of God, that ye may be able to withstand in the evil day, and having done all, to stand.

Ephesians 6:10-13

We do have an enemy, and we must understand him. One of the things military men concentrate on in their training and preparation for battle is knowing the enemy. Even in sports, when a game is to be played against an opposing team, one of the important elements of preparation for the game is to study the opposing team members to know what they are like and how they play. There is an important truth here for every Christian. We must not be ignorant of Satan's devices.

When I teach, I take this need to understand Satan into consideration. I realize that I must spend some time exposing Satan for what he is, and I do this. I never go overboard with this, however, as many seem to be doing these days. If I have thirty minutes to teach, I may use five minutes of that time to expose the devil, but I always use the other twenty-five minutes to talk about God. It is wrong to exalt the problem above the solution.

It doesn't take long to expose the devil, and when he is exposed, we know that we have nothing to fear from him. True, Satan has his own kingdom, but it is a kingdom of darkness and confusion. He no longer has great power. He is merely an imitator, a counterfeiter of God. He tries to imitate everything about God.

God and Satan are opposites. God is a giver, and Satan is a thief. Jesus came *"that [we] might have life,"* and Satan comes *"to steal, to kill, and to destroy"* (John 10:10). God inhabits people for good, and Satan would like to do it for evil. God is constantly searching for someone to bless (see 2 Chronicles 16:9), and Satan is doing just the opposite. He is searching for someone to *"devour"* (1 Peter 5:8).

Using his corrupted wisdom, Satan attempts to come against us and deceive us into believing his lies. If we know what we are dealing with, it makes our warfare against him much easier.

Satan is a deceiver. Believing the truth sets us free, but believing deceptions has the potential to place us into bondage. Those who believe Satan's lies will end up in captivity to him.

Don't let Satan fool you. He is defeated. When Jesus took all of our sins on the cross and when He conquered Hell and Death, He gave Satan a terrible blow:

> *Which he wrought in Christ, when he raised him from the dead, and set him at his own right hand in the heavenly places, far above all principality, and power, and might, and dominion, and every name that is named, not only in this world, but also in that which is to come: and hath put all things under his feet, and gave him to be the head over all things to the church.*
>
> Ephesians 1:20-22

It was at this point that Jesus gave us power and authority over the devil, and we can cast out demons and heal the sick. This infuriates Satan, but he is powerless to stop it. It is part of his continuing judgment.

This, of course, does not mean that Satan is dead or idle. Just the opposite is true. He still hurls his fiery darts at us. He still tries to work on our minds to see if some seed of unbelief can take root, some root of depression, some element of fear. If we recognize and understand his methods, that gives us a great advantage over him.

One thing we can say for Satan is that he is persistent. He never seems to tire, and he comes to us by day and by night, again and again. As long as we are alive in this world, he will feel that he still has a chance to corrupt us, and so he must try.

We can overcome him, as Christians of every century have before us:

> *And they overcame him by the blood of the Lamb, and by the word of their testimony; and they loved not their lives unto the death.*
>
> Revelation 12:11

Since the mind is the area where Satan attacks us, we must constantly be aware of the need to protect ourselves by renewing our minds by filling them with the Word of God. This is our most effective protection from such attacks.

Many Christians have yet to understand the need for this. When we are born again, our spirits are made perfect, but our minds are a long way from perfect. Our thoughts have been formed over a period of years by what we hear and read, and often the influences that formed our thought patterns were not righteous ones. We must, therefore, start a process of renewing our way of thinking.

The first element in this process is a cleansing of our former thought processes. Before we can learn the truth, we must rid our minds of every false thought, every thought that is not in agreement with the Word of God. Only then can we can begin building on the truth.

Renewing our minds is a lot like housecleaning, but it is a radical housecleaning. We must somehow stop thinking our own thoughts and begin thinking God's thoughts. This is not as easy as it might sound. His thoughts are contrary to our thoughts. His ways are contrary to the ways of the world to which we have become accustomed. The ways of the world seem logical to us, and the ways of God do not.

A renewing of our minds will affect every other part of our beings. This, too, is important. We are called to be the very temple of God. He has chosen to dwell in us, and this requires that some changes occur in our way of living so that we present to Him a worthy "house."

When Jesus walked the earth, He was dedicated to driving evil out wherever He saw it. This was not just true the day He went into the Temple in Jerusalem and drove out the money changers who had polluted the Temple with their corrupt business practices. He drove out demons and sickness and sin everywhere He went. And He wants to work this process in us as well.

But what is clear is that we will prevail over Satan and his feeble attempts to defeat us. Jesus said:

> *And I say also unto thee, That thou art Peter, and upon this rock I will build my church; and the gates of hell shall not prevail against it. And I will give unto thee the keys of the kingdom of heaven: and whatsoever thou shalt bind on earth shall be bound in heaven: and whatsoever thou shalt loose on earth shall be loosed in heaven.*
>
> Matthew 16:18-19

Not only has the Lord declared that *"the gates of Hell shall not prevail against [us],"* but He has given us *"the keys of the kingdom of Heaven."* Praise God!

So, what should our attitude be toward Satan?

> *Be sober, be vigilant; because your adversary the devil, as a roaring lion, walketh about, seeking*

whom he may devour: whom resist stedfast in the faith, knowing that the same afflictions are accomplished in your brethren that are in the world. But the God of all grace, who hath called us unto his eternal glory by Christ Jesus, after that ye have suffered a while, make you perfect, stablish, strengthen, settle you.   1 Peter 5:8-10

This is the ultimate slap in the face to Satan. His attempts to destroy us are only working for our good. The pressures he brings can only strengthen us as we overcome them. What an awesome truth! What Satan intends for evil, God is using for our good.

I find that the situation of the children of Israel when they finally reached the Promised Land was very similar to ours today. God had already given them the land, and so it was legally theirs. Interestingly enough, however, they had to go in and take it. If they would believe God and act on His word, the land would be theirs, but they would have to drive out the enemies who were dwelling in the land.

Sometimes that was not as easy as it sounds. Some of these enemies were quite intimidating. There were giants in the land.

What do these giants represent for us? They were types and shadows of any opposition or any problem that we encounter as we move forward to receive what God has promised us. They represented sickness and disease, poverty, personal loss and discouragement. All of these must be driven out if we are to gain the Promised Land.

This is why I love the story of David and Goliath. Many adults fail to appreciate the full meaning of this story, and consider it to be only a story to teach our children and grandchildren. It is much more. It is a wonderful illustration of how our enemy operates against us and of how very easy it is for us to gain the upper hand, when we stay on God's side.

Goliath was called *"a champion"* by his people, and the reason was that he was so very big (1 Samuel 17:4). He was apparently nine or ten feet tall. At the very least, he was bigger than anybody else around.

As if the mere size of this giant was not enough, he also had sophisticated armor and weaponry. The head of his spear weighed more than twenty pounds.

On top of all this, Goliath was adept at bully tactics. He loved to intimidate other men, and he loved to pick a fight, especially since he was bigger than anyone else. King Saul was a big man himself and a professional soldier, but even he was afraid of this giant of a man. And so were all the other soldiers in Israel.

Goliath was very much like the devil:

And the Philistine drew near morning and evening, and presented himself forty days.

1 Samuel 17:16

Imagine him doing this continually over a period of forty days. This is that persistence we were talking about. Satan has a rewind button, and it works very well. He never tires of repeating the same threats over and over and over again.

Satan has another tool. He knows our areas of weakness, and he never fails to rehearse them to us. He does it morning, noon and night, and then he does it again the next day. He is very good at downplaying our strengths and emphasizing our weaknesses.

"I know you got healed five years ago, and what a glorious healing it was; but you're not going to get it this time." Then he repeats those simple words of doubt and unbelief morning, noon and night today, and morning, noon and night tomorrow. This is his *modus operandi.*

I'm so glad that God chose David to defeat this great giant. As we have seen, He is choosing weak vessels to show forth His mighty power in the earth. David was not a professional soldier in any sense of the word; he was a shepherd.

David had gone to see how his brothers were faring in the battle, and he just happened to arrive at a time when Goliath was doing his little stage show to frighten everyone. Little David overheard the uncircumcised Philistine, and he couldn't believe what he was hearing. He knew God's covenant as none other seemed to know it at the moment. Even Saul, who was head and shoulders above all the other soldiers of Israel, was terrified of the giant.

Something welled up within David's spirit and he asked, *"Who is this uncircumcised Philistine, that he should defy the armies of the living God?"* (1 Samuel 17:26). That sounded like pride to his brothers, and they accused him of arrogance. "Why don't you go back to your few sheep," they taunted. "What do you have to be so proud about?" Faith often sounds like pride to those who don't understand what you are saying. On another occasion, David sang:

> *My soul shall make her boast in the LORD:*
> *the humble shall hear thereof, and be glad.*
>
> Psalm 34:2

But David was not making his boast in himself; he was making it *"in the Lord."* The prideful may not have found reason to rejoice in this, but *"the humble"* did.

So here was a young kid with no experience whatsoever in warfare, and suddenly he is pitted against the mighty champion warrior giant. Isn't that astonishing? It seems ridiculous, doesn't it? And it seems just as ridiculous to say that we should never fear Satan, but that is the truth.

David wasn't afraid, because he had proven God to

be true. When a lion and a bear (on two different occasions) threatened to do harm to the flocks he was guarding, he rose up and killed them both. Now, he predicted:

> *The LORD that delivered me out of the paw of the lion, and out of the paw of the bear, he will deliver me out of the hand of this Philistine.*
>
> 1 Samuel 17:37

Saul reluctantly agreed for David to fight the giant, but he tried to put his armor on the lad. It was so heavy, however, that David couldn't move around with it on. He wasn't trusting in armor anyway, and he wasn't trusting in himself. God had chosen him to fight the battle, so he was trusting in the goodness of God.

David picked up five small stones, and he went forward toward the enemy lines. What he said as he approached this mighty giant should encourage us all:

> *Then said David to the Philistine, Thou comest to me with a sword, and with a spear, and with a shield: but I come to thee in the name of the LORD of hosts, the God of the armies of Israel, whom thou hast defied. This day will the LORD deliver thee into mine hand; and I will smite thee, and*

> *take thine head from thee; and I will give the car-*
> *cases of the host of the Philistines this day unto*
> *the fowls of the air, and to the wild beasts of the*
> *earth; that all the earth may know that there is a*
> *God in Israel. And all this assembly shall know*
> *that the LORD saveth not with sword and spear:*
> *for the battle is the LORD'S, and he will give you*
> *into our hands.*   1 Samuel 17:45-47

This is how the Lord does it, and it is how He has always done it. Stop allowing the enemy to intimidate you. If you are weak, so much the better. God delights in bringing victories through the weakest vessels among us. It's not wrong to recognize your weakness, but it is wrong to fear the enemy when Almighty God is with you.

It wasn't a sling or a stone that killed Goliath. It was the power of the Holy Ghost in a small lad. It must have been an amusing sight as David took up the huge sword of the giant and used it to cut the "champion's" head off with.

What are you facing today and tomorrow? Know that *"the battle is the Lord's."* As members of the Body of Christ, we have a glorious future. What devil can stand in the presence of the living God? What devil is to be considered when we know that Jesus is with us? He has done the work on Calvary. He rose from the grave, conquering Hell and Death. He is now living as our High Priest. Satan has been disarmed, bound and gagged, and left naked and exposed. All that remains is to take the devil's own sword and cut his head off.

No weapon formed against us will prosper. These assignments of Hell that we overcome will only make us stronger. What an awesome God we serve. This is our present status, *After the Cross*. As we come to know Jesus in the power of His resurrection, victory is ours.

Chapter Twenty-Three

What About Spiritual Warfare?

For though we walk in the flesh, we do not war after the flesh: (for the weapons of our warfare are not carnal, but mighty through God to the pulling down of strong holds;) casting down imaginations, and every high thing that exalteth itself against the knowledge of God, and bringing into captivity every thought to the obedience of Christ.

2 Corinthians 10:3-5

During the time the Lord was revealing to me the depths of His sacrifice on Calvary and the ministry He is performing for us now as our High Priest, I said to Him, "If You have already defeated Satan (and that's what the message of the Gospel is), how can I reconcile all the warfare scriptures in the Bible?" I believed in spiritual warfare, and I had been doing quite a bit of ministry on that subject. Now, I was having a hard time reconciling the two teachings. The Lord showed me that if we do not take the teachings of spiritual warfare to their extreme, we are correct to teach it and practice it.

I am convinced, for instance, that healing – both receiving healing and ministering healing to others – comes through spiritual warfare. After all, Satan is the author of sickness and disease. When we receive healing or minister it to others, we are coming against the power of Satan and defeating him through the cross.

Part of Jesus' ministry was to do warfare with Satan:

> *How God anointed Jesus of Nazareth with the Holy Ghost and with power: who went about doing good, and healing all that were oppressed of the devil; for God was with him.*
>
> Acts 10:38

This same ministry of spiritual warfare has been given to us to fulfill, and we have been given authority and the tools necessary to fulfill it.

This term *"pulling down"* is important to us. In the very next verse, Paul said: "*Casting down imaginations, and every high thing.*" This means that I am to pull down anything that would exalt itself against the knowledge of God, anything that would exalt itself against the resurrection of Jesus Christ, anything that would attempt to hide or deny what Jesus has already done for us in His death and in His resurrection.

I am convinced that ninety-five percent of our spiritual warfare is done in the mind. That is where Satan attacks us. That is where he plants his seeds of doubt and fear, which is pride. That is where he attempts to insert depression. Whether we like it or not, we are in a warfare.

There are some extreme teachings concerning spiritual warfare, and we must guard ourselves against these. Some people, for instance, overemphasize the devil, and this causes people to be afraid of him. The devil is the focal point of their teachings, and this glorifies him. On the other extreme, there are those who are totally ignorant of the devil or who ignore him. This also is dangerous, because the Scriptures teach us that if we ignore him, he will take advantage of us.

Whatever you do, be careful never to exalt the problem over the solution. The Solution is greater, and His name is Jesus. Your need is never greater than God's capacity to supply it. Your problem is never greater than God's ability to resolve it. Your sickness is never greater than God's ability to heal it.

Satan was the first transgressor, and through his corrupted wisdom, he has become the master of deceit. He is very good at making you believe a lie. The truth will set you free, but Satan's lies will imprison you. Be careful not to be snared by the enemy.

If these teachings still seem unreasonable to you, don't worry about it. Was it reasonable that God could speak the world into existence? Was it reasonable that an old man could have a child after his wife had gone through menopause and had also been barren through what we normally call "the childbearing years"? Was it reasonable to think that a virgin could conceive and bear a child? None of these things were reasonable, but the Holy Spirit brought them all into being. In the same way, He is ready to take bold and powerful statements such as we have been confessing here, put them in our hearts, give us understanding of them, fill out mouths with them and, as we declare them and live them out, bring them to pass.

We are living in a very exciting time, the final hour for the Church. We are about to see the Lord doing the most unusual miracles we could imagine, and using the most unusual people to do them. He is about to be glorified through the humblest vessels among us. In this way, He will receive the greater glory unto Himself.

As we enter this most wonderful time in history, if you will believe God to accomplish in you all that He has provided for, it will be done. Know Jesus in the power of His resurrection. After all, we are living *After the Cross.*

Confessions of My Faith

> *For this cause also thank we God without ceasing, because, when ye received the word of God which ye heard of us, ye received it not as the word of men, but as it is in truth, the word of God, WHICH EFFECTUALLY WORKETH ALSO IN YOU THAT BELIEVE.*
>
> 1 Thessalonians 2:13

It is very important for you as a believer to let the truths of the Word get into your spirit, then into your mouth, and to begin to confess them. I have developed my own personal confessions of my faith based on the promises of God's Word. When I began to make these confessions, I found that they began to work in me – spirit, soul and body. And I have never been the same since. I encourage you to do the same:

- I am in Jesus, and He is in me. (John 14:20)

- He is the vine. I am the branch. I abide in Him and bear much fruit. Without Him I can do nothing. (John 15:5)

- I can do all things in Him. (Philippians 4:13)

- I abide in Him, and His words live in me. (John 15:4-5)

- Because of this, I ask whatever I want and it is done. (John 15:7)

- In Him, I live and move and have my being. (Acts 17:28)

- I have the righteousness of God which is by faith of Jesus Christ. It is unto me and upon me because I believe. (Romans 3:22)

- I am justified [made holy] freely by His grace. (Romans 3:24)

- Being justified, I have peace. (Romans 5:1)

- I have access, by faith, into this grace wherein I stand. (Romans 5:2)

- Because I'm justified, I am saved from wrath. (Romans 5:9)

- I receive abundance of grace and reign in life. (Romans 5:17)

- I was baptized into Jesus Christ and into His death. (Romans 6:3)

- Because I am dead with Him, now I live with Him. (Romans 6:8)

• Christ died to sin for me. (Romans 6:10)

• I consider that I am dead to sin and alive to God. (Romans 6:11)

• There is no condemnation to me, because I walk after the Spirit, not my flesh. (Romans 8:1)

• The Spirit of life in Christ Jesus has made me free from the law of sin and death. (Romans 8:2)

• If God didn't spare His own Son, He won't spare anything. He will freely give me all things. (Romans 8:32)

• I am more than a conqueror. (Romans 8:37)

• In everything I am enriched by Him, in all utterance, in all knowledge. (1 Corinthians 1:5)

• Jesus is made unto me wisdom, and righteousness and sanctification, and redemption. (1 Corinthians 1:30)

• I am joined to the Lord. I am one spirit with Him. (1 Corinthians 6:17)

• My body is the temple of the Lord. I am not my own. (1 Corinthians 6:19)

• I have been bought with a price. My body and my spirit are God's. (1 Corinthians 6:20)

• God gives me the victory in Jesus. (1 Corinthians 15:57)

- God always causes me to triumph in Christ. He reveals Himself through me in every place. (2 Corinthians 2:14)

- I am a new creation. (2 Corinthians 5:17)

- I am the righteousness of God in Christ. (2 Corinthians 5:21)

- I am justified by the faith of Jesus. (Galatians 2:16)

- I am crucified with Christ. I am alive but it is His life. He lives in me. The life I live now, I live by the faith of the Son of God, who loved me and gave Himself for me. (Galatians 2:20)

- Christ redeemed me from the curse of the law [defeat by enemies, sickness and poverty, as in Deuteronomy 28]. (Galatians 3:13)

- The blessing of Abraham is mine and the promise of the Spirit through faith. (Galatians 3:14)

- I am a child of God. (Galatians 3:26)

- I was baptized into Christ. (Galatians 3:27)

- I put on Christ. (Galatians 3:27)

- I am Christ's. I am Abraham's seed and heir. (Galatians 3:29)

- I am a child of God and His heir. (Galatians 4:7)

- The only thing that benefits me is faith that works through love. (Galatians 5:6)

- The world is crucified unto me and I am crucified unto the world. (Galatians 6:14)

- God has already blessed me with all spiritual blessings in heavenly places in Christ. (Ephesians 1:3)

- He has chosen me and I am holy and without blame before Him. (Ephesians 1:4)

- He has made me accepted. (Ephesians 1:6)

- I have redemption and forgiveness of sins. (Ephesians 1:7)

- He has overflowed toward me in all wisdom and prudence. (Ephesians 1:8)

- His power far surpasses being just great toward me. (Ephesians 1:19)

- It is resurrection power. (Ephesians 1:20)

- All things are under my feet. (Ephesians 1:22)

- He made me alive with Christ. (Ephesians 2:5)

- By grace I am saved. (Ephesians 2:5)

- He raised me and made me sit in heavenly places. (Ephesians 2:6)

- He will show that His grace is more, surpassing just

being rich and wealthy, by His kindness to me. (Ephesians 2:7)

• I have bold access to Him, with confidence, by faith. (Ephesians 3:12)

• I am light. (Ephesians 5:8)

• God works in me and causes me to want to do His will and pleasure. (Philippians 2:13)

• I do not worry about anything, because in everything I give my wants and needs to God and He keeps my mind and my heart in peace. (Philippians 4:6-7)

• I can do all things through Him, who strengthens me. (Philippians 4:13)

• My God supplies all my needs and lacks. I shall not want. (Philippians 4:19 and Psalm 23:1)

• He makes me able to receive my inheritance. (Colossians 1:12)

• He has delivered me from all power and control of darkness and put me in the Kingdom of Jesus. (Colossians 1:13)

• I have redemption and forgiveness of sins. (Colossians 1:14

• I was created by Him and for Him. (Colossians 1:16)

- He presents me holy, unblamable and unreproveable in His sight because I continue in the faith. (Colossians 1:22-23)

- I have access to all wisdom and knowledge. (Colossians 2:3)

- I walk in Him as I received Him (by faith). (Colossians 2:6)

- I am rooted and built up in Him, and established in the faith, abounding with thanksgiving. (Colossians 2:7)

- I am complete in Him. (Colossians 2:10)

- I am circumcised in Him [The control the flesh had over me has been cut, I am dead to the flesh by the death of Jesus] and was buried with Him. (Colossians 2:11-12)

- I am risen with Him. (Colossians 2:12)

- God made me alive with Him. (Colossians 2:13)

- He forgave me all. (Colossians 2:13)

- Since I am risen with Him, I seek only those things above. (Colossians 3:1)

- My affections [desires] are set on things above. (Colossians 3:2)

- I am dead, and my life is hid with Christ. (Colossians 3:3)

- The grace of my God is exceedingly abundant with faith and love. (1 Timothy 1:14)

- I hold His words in faith and love. (2 Timothy 1:13)

- I am strong in His grace. (2 Timothy 2:1)

- Christ, by His own blood, entered into the Holy Place and obtained redemption for me. (Hebrews 9:11-12)

- I have boldness to enter into the Holiest Place by the blood of Jesus. (Hebrews 10:19)

- My God works through the blood in me, making me perfect in every good work, to do His will, working in me that which is well pleasing in His sight through Jesus Christ. (Hebrews 13:21)

- I have not seen Him, but I love Him. (1 Peter 1:8)

- I know when I'm believing because when I am believing, I rejoice with joy unspeakable and full of glory. (1 Peter 1:8)

- I am a living stone built into His dwelling place. (1 Peter 2:5)

- I offer up to Him spiritual sacrifices [praises] acceptable to God. (1 Peter 2:5)

- If I keep His word, His love is perfected in me. [This is how I know I am in Him.] (1 John 2:5)

- I can have forgiveness, in the measure I forgive (Matthew 6:12 and 14), mercy, in the measure I give mercy (James 2:12-13 and Psalm 18:25) and material blessings, in the measure I give (Luke 6:38).

- I will reap back, multiplied over, anything I sow [forgiveness, love, mercy, money, etc.]. (Galatians 6:7 and Luke 6:3)

- The anointing I received abides in me and teaches and reveals Him unto me. (1 John 2:27 and Hebrews 8:11)

- God's covenant with me is that I will know Him. (Hebrews 8:11)

- Because I know Him, I love the brethren. (1 John 4:7-8)

- As I walk in love, His love is perfected in me. (1 John 4:12)

- So, I will never fail! (1 Corinthians 13:8)

Ministry address:

Sara Gibson
Sara Gibson Ministry
Post Office Box 4404
Meridian, MS 39304

SGibson7@aol.com